Political Participation in Britain

CONTEMPORARY POLITICAL STUDIES SERIES

Series Editor: John Benyon, University of Leicester

Contemporary Political Studies Series

Series Standing Order ISBN 978–0–230–54350–8 hardback
Series Standing Order ISBN 978–0–230–54351–5 paperback
(outside North America only)

You can receive future titles in this series as they are published by placing a standing
order. Please contact your bookseller or, in case of difficulty, write to us at the address
below with your name and address, the title of the series and one of the ISBNs quoted
above.

Customer Services Department, Macmillan Distribution Ltd
Houndmills, Basingstoke, Hampshire RG21 6XS, England, UK

Political Participation in Britain

The Decline and Revival of Civic Culture

Paul Whiteley

First published 2012 by
PALGRAVE MACMILLAN

Palgrave Macmillan in the UK is an imprint of Macmillan Publishers Limited, registered in England, company number 785998, of Houndmills, Basingstoke, Hampshire RG21 6XS.

Palgrave Macmillan in the US is a division of St Martin's Press LLC, 175 Fifth Avenue, New York, NY 10010.

Palgrave Macmillan is the global academic imprint of the above companies and has companies and representatives throughout the world.

Palgrave® and Macmillan® are registered trademarks in the United States, the United Kingdom, Europe and other countries

ISBN 978-1-4039-4265-4   hardback
ISBN 978-1-4039-4266-1   paperback

This book is printed on paper suitable for recycling and made from fully managed and sustained forest sources. Logging, pulping and manufacturing processes are expected to conform to the environmental regulations of the country of origin.

A catalogue record for this book is available from the British Library.

A catalog record for this book is available from the Library of Congress.

10 9 8 7 6 5 4 3 2 1
21 20 19 18 17 16 15 14 13 12

Printed and bound in China

To Ava and Sophia

Contents

List of Figures

List of Tables

Acknowledgements

This book has been more than ten years in the making. This was not the original plan when Steve Kennedy from Palgrave Macmillan suggested it to Pat Seyd and myself, but that is how it turned out. The usual excuses apply, namely that we had many other commitments, in my case to the British Election Study, and when Pat retired he wanted a break from academic writing, so the project was recast as a single-authored text. In the end, the time lag proved to be something of a silver lining since it was possible to make use of a lot more comparative survey data, which has increasingly become available in recent years, to examine Britain's position among the advanced industrial democracies. My thanks go to colleagues for many intellectual exchanges over the years, all of which really help the thinking and writing processes. These include Pat Seyd, Harold Clarke, Marianne Stewart, David Sanders and Charles Pattie. Particular thanks go to Steve Kennedy for his patience in the face of my tardiness.

PAUL WHITELEY

Boxford, Suffolk

Preface

The aim of this book is to examine the relationship between civil society, democracy and government in contemporary Britain. It looks at the extent to which the state relies on political participation and the key institutions of civil society, such as political parties, interest groups and voluntary organizations, in order to govern effectively. It also explores the evolving relationship between political participation and the attitudes and values of citizens, which underpins civil society and the British state. It traces political attitudes and behaviour in Britain from the 1950s through to contemporary times, highlighting the most significant changes that have occurred. It also assesses the implications of these changes for contemporary British government and democracy.

The analysis in the book ranges across an investigation of what people think and what they do when acting as citizens, and how these link to the overall problem of governing effectively in the twenty-first century. It is a complex story involving an examination of attitudes to government and policy making, beliefs about the institutions of civil society such as political parties, and also the extent that people participate both in politics and in wider voluntary activities in society. It looks closely at voting and other forms of political participation, seeking to explain why people should participate in politics in the first place. It then looks at the relationship between civic engagement and the civic culture and governance.

There are two overarching themes developed in the book. The first is the theme of understanding and mapping out the dimensions of civil society in contemporary Britain. This involves asking questions such as:

- How has democracy been defined and practised in Britain?
- To what extent have political values and attitudes changed among the public over time?
- To what extent has political participation changed and if it has, why has this happened?
- How exceptional is Britain in comparison with other established democracies?

These are important questions and they are addressed with the help of a great deal of evidence from diverse sources.

The second broad theme asks what difference does civil society and civic engagement make to government and policy making? Addressing this involves looking at such questions as:

• Does voluntary activity help to improve policy delivery?
• Does citizen participation in politics produce better government?
• Is British democracy improving or deteriorating?

It is fair to say that this second theme has been relatively neglected in comparison with the first. While it has always been assumed that a vibrant civic culture is good for democracy and government, it has not often been clearly demonstrated. Of course, a healthy democracy is a good thing in its own right and does not have to be justified in wider terms. But as this book will show, it can be justified in a wider setting, because it is clear that an effective democracy delivers effective government; civil society and good government are intimately related.

The civic culture, even though it is often taken for granted, is of central importance in influencing politics and government – in some ways the civic culture determines the constitution and anchors British democracy. Governments of particular political persuasions get into power because they are elected by the general public, yet they can only carry out their programme of government with the continued support of the public. Policy proposals are always made with an eye on public opinion, and governing always involves making choices against a background of what the public want, or are willing to put up with. Policy u-turns, for example, seldom arise from a careful reasoned analysis of the alternatives, and are much more likely to be triggered by a public outcry in reaction to whatever is being proposed. Similarly, with a few exceptions, successful policies work because they are supported by the majority of the population who reluctantly accept them at worst and actively help to implement them at best. The role of the law, acting to sanction people in enforcing policies, is greatly exaggerated, although it does have a place. Successful policies are supported and facilitated by the public as a whole, which is one of the reasons why they are successful.

So the core thesis of this book is that a healthy civil society makes for good governance and effective policy making. But there are warning clouds on the horizon, since civil society in Britain is not as healthy as it was a generation ago. Civic engagement is in decline, public attitudes and values are less supportive of governance than they once were and as a consequence the effectiveness of government is waning. Britain is in danger of becoming a 'flawed democracy' (a concept discussed in detail in Chapter 9). This theme runs through the book, but in the final chapter I explore some options designed to change this state of affairs for the better and to revive civic engagement in Britain.

The general election of 2010 was a turning point in post-war British politics since it produced the first full coalition government since the Second World War. This came about because no party obtained a majority of seats in the House of Commons and so an accommodation between political parties had to be reached. This is obvious enough, but it raises an interesting question: why did no party get an overall majority, when up to that point Britain had experienced nothing but single-party governments since the Second World War? The answer to this question can be found in trends in the civic culture and in political participation which have slowly been evolving behind the scenes for years. These trends, which are discussed extensively in this book, came to a head in the 2010 general election to produce a dramatic change in the nature of British government. This is a clear example of how the civic culture directly affects politics and government and will continue to do so in the future.

1

British Democracy in the Twenty-First Century

The political culture in Great Britain also approximates the civic culture. The participant role is highly developed. Exposure to politics, interest, involvement, and a sense of competence are relatively high. There are norms supporting political activity, as well as emotional involvement in elections, and system affect. And the attachment to the system is a balanced one: there is general system pride as well as satisfaction with specific government performance. (Almond and Verba, 1963: 315)

Popular engagement with the formal processes and institutions of democracy has been in long-term decline since the 1960s. Party memberships have been falling continuously since that time to the point where they stand at less that one-quarter of their 1964 levels. The number of people who say they identify with one of the main parties has followed a similar severe trajectory. Turnout for other elections – local and European parliamentary – have remained stubbornly low for decades. (Power to the People, 2006: 27)

These two descriptions of the state of civil society in Britain are separated by nearly fifty years. The first comes from the classic study of participation by Almond and Verba undertaken in 1959. The second is from the report of the Power Commission, an investigation of the state of democracy in Britain published in 2006. There is a dramatic difference between these two accounts of British democracy. The aim of this book is to explain why these changes have occurred and what they mean for British politics and society.

This is a book about citizenship and civil society, that is, relationships between ordinary people and between the citizens of Britain and their governments. Civil society is the foundation upon which democracy and effective government are built, so the scope of the analysis and its implications are wide. We will look at the norms and values that underpin democracy, at political participation broadly defined, at voluntary activity and civic engagement and, after mapping out the contours of civil society, assess its effects on governance and society. As well as describing the characteristics of civil society in contemporary Britain, we also look at changes that have occurred in civic engagement and political values over time. In addition, the book considers Britain in a comparative context to see how it appears in relation to other advanced industrial democracies. Finally, we will examine what can be done to offset some of the trends identified, which are generally not beneficial for democracy and wider British society.

Civic engagement is essentially about ordinary citizens trying to influence the policies and the personnel of the state, thus the relationship between the state and participation is central to the analysis. We know that key forms of participation such as voting and party membership have declined significantly (Seyd and Whiteley, 2002; Clarke *et al.*, 2004, 2009). At the same time, other forms of participation, such as consumer involvement in buying or boycotting products for political reasons, are growing in importance (Pattie, Seyd and Whiteley, 2004). Unfortunately, voting is much more important for democracy than boycotting, since it determines who governs the state, and these developments have not left the civic culture undamaged.

An earlier comprehensive study of civic attitudes and behaviour in contemporary Britain (Pattie, Seyd and Whiteley, 2004) found that people's sense of citizenship is deeply embedded. The British are a law-abiding people and they possess a sense of civic obligation, for example, they believe that they should pay their taxes, they should serve on a jury when required, and they should give blood. However, some of the key features of Almond and Verba's (1963) British civic culture of the 1960s have today most definitely changed. They are less trusting of their government and the institutions of the state such as Parliament, and they are less likely to look out for their fellow citizens. Civic culture in early twenty-first century Britain differs markedly from that which prevailed in the mid-twentieth century.

The civic culture extolled by Almond and Verba was based upon a long-standing tradition of parliamentary democracy. We begin the analysis by looking at the prevailing constitutional doctrines that govern British politics, since this is a key backdrop for understanding civil society and civic engagement. In this chapter we will outline the essential features of British parliamentary democracy and then consider why this form of democracy no longer seems so appropriate to many people's needs and expectations in twenty-first century Britain. A constitution which worked well in the post-war years is looking increasingly threadbare and ineffective, and this links into to the findings later on in this book.

British parliamentary democracy: theory and practice

As British democracy steadily evolved from the seventeenth century onwards it was based upon the two key principles of representation and accountability (Birch, 1964; Judge, 1993,1999). Both of these principles have various meanings. As far as representation is concerned, Birch (1964: 16) notes that the term representative can mean an agent or delegate acting on behalf of a particular group, or a trustee obliged in some way to advance the interests of such a group, or alternatively a person who has the typical characteristics of the members of the group. Historically, representation in Britain has referred primarily to the trustee role rather than the delegate role or that of a typical person.

With regard to accountability or responsibility, this can mean government responsiveness to public demands, or alternatively the pursuit of what government considers wise policies irrespective of short-term public opinion. Birch states that responsibility in Britain means 'first, consistency, prudence and leadership, second, accountability to Parliament and the electorate, and third, responsiveness to public opinion and demands' (1964: 245) in that order of importance. The prevailing sense of these two principles of representation and accountability, therefore, has been to limit public influence on the day-to-day process of government. British democracy has been very much a 'top-down' affair with the emphasis being placed upon leadership rather than mass participation. This, in part, is a legacy of monarchical autocracy which existed in a much earlier era.

Election has been the principal means of achieving both representation and accountability. Through the nineteenth and twentieth centuries, the political elite conceded that the public was increasingly qualified to participate in elections and therefore the franchise was gradually extended. First, it was extended from a minority to a majority of property holders, and subsequently from a limited proportion of male manual workers to all of them. Eventually it was given to women over the age of 30 and finally to women over 21. Surprisingly enough the first general election in which all adults over the age of 21 were eligible to vote was in 1931. This state of affairs continued until 1970 when electoral eligibility was redefined as those aged 18 and over.

The essential feature of this enfranchised mass electorate was that all who participated had an equal voice 'one person, one vote' irrespective of wealth, power, or knowledge. Notwithstanding the considerable social and economic inequalities in British society, equality prevailed at the ballot box. Thus socialist and renowned left-wing Labour MP

Aneurin Bevan wrote that '[t]he function of parliamentary democracy, under universal franchise ... is to expose wealth-privilege to the attack of the people' (1952: 5). At five-yearly intervals the British political elite was forced to justify itself to the common man and woman, and in between times it had to defend itself before an elected parliament.

Notwithstanding this egalitarian democratic principle, British democracy in practice has been elitist, in the sense that the operation of government has restricted popular input. Apart from the public's periodic participation in electing the members of the House of Commons from whom governments have been selected, its engagement in government has been minimal. This is epitomized by the crown prerogative, which sanctifies executive power, and reinforces the notion of Britons as subjects not citizens. 'His' or 'Her' Majesty's Government possesses extensive powers to act with very few restraints. Only in 2000 was a Human Rights Act introduced, which, for the very first time, gave individuals statutory rights against executive power. Furthermore, although the day-to-day business of government requires the approval of the House of Commons, the public's representatives, the elected members of the House of Commons, are trustees rather than delegates. So the representatives have been elected to use their independent judgement and have not been bound by instructions from their electors and, as a consequence, have been insulated from majority public opinion. Representatives have exercised their powers ultimately in the interests of the represented, but the represented have been afforded little direct say in the determination of public policy. Even when referendums have been used, as they have on a number of occasions since 1975, the results have not been formally binding upon parliament.

As representative democracy developed in the nineteenth and twentieth centuries so did programmatic parties (Beer, 1965). Parties presented their programmes in the form of manifestos to the electorate. The doctrine is that voters are assumed to make an informed choice of a party on the basis of these programmes and the successful party then translates its programme into practice once in government. Party discipline in the House of Commons ensures that a governing party's programme is implemented. The party is then judged by the voters on its success in implementing its promises at the subsequent election. In the face of political opposition from within the House of Commons or from the unelected House of Lords, or from particular interests or sections of the population, elections provided a governing party with a sense of mandate to counter such opposition and proceed with its proposals. This 'responsible' party system ensures both political accountability and governmental coherence. These two qualities were the reason why a group of US political scientists (APSA, 1950) recommended that a 'responsible' party system should be introduced into their country as a means of improving the quality of the governing process.

Accountability has been implemented in the British system primarily through the opportunity provided by elections for the voters 'to kick the rascals out' and by the institutionalization of an Opposition and therefore the existence of an alternative government in waiting ready to take on the responsibilities of power. In addition, however, between elections, a dialogue takes place between governments and the governed, partly through elected MPs, but also through interest and pressure groups. From the nineteenth century onwards specific interests organized themselves to ensure that their particular point of view might be articulated, and by the early twentieth century they were being consulted by governments (Beer, 1965; Middlemas, 1986). As the twentieth century progressed so the number of interest and pressure groups steadily grew and they became part of a continual conversation between rulers and the ruled.

Some tensions existed between mass public and elite opinions on specific issues such as the levels of immigration into Britain in the 1950s, the abolition of capital punishment for murder, the amount of money devoted to military defence expenditure during the Cold War, and Britain's entry into the European Economic Community. Nevertheless, levels of public support for this political system were high in the mid-century. Almond and Verba (1963) argue that Britain possessed a balanced civic culture in which people were neither too active nor too passive. People's levels of system satisfaction were high. They were proud of their political institutions and system of government, and they believed that they received equal treatment from government and considerateness and responsiveness from bureaucrats. Their sense of political competence, influence and interest, and their levels of political participation, were relatively high, and the British trusted one another. Overall, the quote from Almond and Verba at the start of this chapter summarizes the position in the late 1950s and early 1960s.

To what extent were Almond and Verba correct in their judgement of British civic culture? Maybe 1959, the year in which they conducted their survey, was an exceptional one, an 'annus mirabilis' in terms of civic life, and was an outlier therefore in terms of post-war civic attitudes? There may be particular features of the late 1950s which exaggerated the sense of civic culture among the British. For example, the growth in personal living standards is one factor. Prime Minister Harold

Macmillan won the 1959 general election with the slogan 'Most people have never had it so good' reflecting the growing post-war affluence (Butler and Rose, 1959). Times of growing prosperity might make citizens more optimistic and less critical than otherwise. Dennis Kavanagh (1980) in particular has argued that their methodology was flawed, pointing out that the response rate to their survey among the British was low (56 per cent) compared with the Americans (83 per cent), the Germans (74 per cent), and the Italians (74 per cent). The low British response rate might mean that critical and dissatisfied citizens are absent from the sample, thereby containing a disproportionate number of politically active, satisfied individuals. These queries are very difficult to resolve, but we do know from a survey conducted in October 1968, nearly ten years after Almond and Verba were in the field, that only 41 per cent of respondents to a Gallup Poll agreed that the 'present parliamentary system is satisfactory', while 44 per cent disagreed (King, Wybrow and Gallup, 2000: 285). So it is possible that Almond and Verba exaggerated to some extent the effectiveness of the British political system.

Challenges to British parliamentary democracy

What is clear is that from the 1960s onwards the public were growing increasingly critical of the performance of governments. This is apparent from Figure 1.1 which shows levels of approval of successive governments over a period of forty-five years from 1960 to 2005. The data is derived from a question regularly asked by Gallup: 'Do you approve or disapprove of the Government's record to date?' (King, Wybrow and Gallup, 2000: 167–7). The chart shows a fairly rapid increase in dissatisfaction with Government performance during the 1970s compared with earlier. Of course there were particular circumstances associated with the Conservative government of Edward Heath from 1970 to 1974, and again the minority Labour government after 1974 which helped to bring this about, but it is noticeable that approval ratings never returned to the level of the 1960s even during the period following Labour's landslide victory in 1997. British citizens are relatively dissatisfied with the performance of their governments in comparison with an earlier era, something which is true regardless of their political makeup.

After the 1970s, a less deferential public was making increased demands on governments for the delivery of good public services and improved standards of living. At the same time both the Conservative

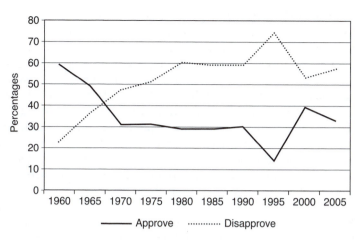

Source: King, Wybrow and Gallup, 2000 and IPSOS-MORI, http://www.ipsos.com/.7.

Figure 1.1   Trends in approval and disapproval of government, 1960 to 2005

and Labour parties' traditional class sources of electoral support were being eroded, a topic we examine in Chapter 3. If the voters' attachment to their political parties is weak then they are much less likely to tolerate what they see as failure and much more willing to switch to another party if things start to go wrong in government. The combination of these two factors produced an inflationary spiral of political expectations and demands, and of party promises and commitments (Beer, 1982), which no party is able to satisfy. Thus the capacity of governments to deliver has declined, a topic we return to in Chapter 8. Governing parties' dependency upon other institutions, both national and international to deliver (poor leadership in some cases) combined with increasing levels of public cynicism about government meant that they could not satisfy public demands.

Criticisms of the two key principles of parliamentary democracy – representation and accountability – and of the most important political institutions grew in the last two decades of the twentieth century (Weir and Beetham, 1999). These criticisms were most comprehensively outlined in Weir and Beetham's *Democratic Audit*. Critics argued that representation was being distorted by an electoral system that accentuated two-party, and restricted minor-party, support (Weir and Beetham, 1999: 45–79). Representation was also being undermined by political marketing as parties no longer provided electors with meaningful choices.

Their manifestos were bland, public-relations exercises mainly aimed at attracting an electoral majority rather than translating public opinions into government actions. Furthermore, there was no guarantee that governing parties would implement their manifesto promises and it often became the case that they put into practice, those things that they had promised not to do in their manifestos (Weir and Beetham, 1999: 100–15). After the election of a Labour government in 1997 the criticism that public accountability was being undermined by political marketing was even stronger. The government's extensive control of, and influence upon, public information was being used to fabricate and manipulate public opinion. Government 'spin', or manipulation of opinion, became a common word in everyday political discussions.

Another criticism was that the principle of democratic equality had been undermined by the parties' dependence upon corporate donors. Politics had become so expensive and the two major parties had become so dependent upon a small number of rich financial donors that the egalitarian democratic principle had become fatally undermined. Financial support guaranteed preferential access to governments and, on occasions, unduly influenced policy outcomes. This arose, in part, because of the decline of the voluntary party organizations, an issue which is examined in more detail in Chapter 4.

A further problem has been the growth in dissatisfaction with the effectiveness of Parliament in Britain. In the 2001 election study survey respondents were asked to indicate if they respected Parliament using a zero to ten scale where zero meant they had no respect at all and ten meant they had complete respect. The mean score in 2001 was 5.5, but by 2010 using a similar scale in which respondents were asked about trust in Parliament the mean score had fallen to 4.7. The two scales are not exactly the same, but they hint at a growing lack of respect for, and trust in, Parliament. Since Parliament in general and the House of Commons in particular is the central focus of the British Constitution this is clearly a problem. In fairness, citizens are more favourably inclined towards their own MP than politicians in general. In the 2005 election study survey 50 per cent of people agreed with the statement that: 'My member of Parliament works hard to try and look after the interests of people who live in my constituency' (only 17 per cent disagreed). Notwithstanding this point there is a generalized mistrust of politicians.

Defenders of the status quo typically respond that institutional reform is something that only excites 'the chattering class' while most people remained unconcerned about constitutional matters and institutional reforms. To a large extent this is true but, nonetheless, the Labour government embarked on limited constitutional changes after 1997 with devolution to Scotland and Wales and initial reform of the House of Lords. These changes have shown that constitutional reform does alter the way that citizens perceive and relate to their governments. The Parliaments in Edinburgh and Cardiff are now an integral part of the Scottish and Welsh political landscapes and significant policy differences have appeared between these countries and England. It is now unthinkable for these Parliaments to be wound up and the constitutional changes reversed, and indeed there is pressure for greater devolution in both countries. Thus constitutional reform has changed British politics and opened up new possibilities for governance and civil society. Reform of Britain's political institutions was demanded by various groups, including the newly formed Charter Movement and the long-established Electoral Reform Society. The coalition government elected in 2010 embarked on a referendum on electoral reform, largely in response to demands from the Liberal Democrats, but its failure to pass, when the referendum was held in May 2011, has shut down that particular avenue of reform for the foreseeable future.

So the background developments in government and in the institutions of the state over time have served to make citizens increasingly critical, less trusting and less deferential towards the state and public authorities in Britain. As we shall see later this is making government work less effectively, and so changes in the civic culture have concrete effects for British politics. In the next section we examine the relationship between democracy and civil society, the central theme of this book.

Democracy and civil society

Democracy is a system of government in which 'who gets what, when and how' (Lasswell, 1936) is settled by deliberation and agreement. Representative democracy does not require its citizens to participate in politics on a daily basis, but it does require them to participate on important occasions, for example, when their elected representatives are chosen at the ballot box. If few people participate in elections, then the state will lose its legitimacy and it will not be able to persuade its citizens to cooperate in the tasks of governing. Given that a good deal of policy making in the modern state requires persuasion rather than coercion, this is likely to undermine the effectiveness of government. In those circumstances, government is likely to be seen as oppressive, meddling and irrelevant to the everyday needs of the average person, since it will not be responsive or accountable to them.

Similarly, democracy does not require universal agreement about policies, but it does need individuals to be reconciled to decisions which go against them. If nothing can be settled because losers in the policy-making process refuse to accept decisions, then democracy will become paralysed. Decisions have to be made and if powerful minorities refuse to accept majority preferences, or equally if majorities systematically ignore the interests of minorities and exclude them from the political process, then there will be no closure to politics. The result is likely to be policy gridlock and conflict.

A further point is that democracy does not require citizens to like each other, but it does require them to tolerate different views, since the reconciliation of disagreements without force is the essence of democratic decision making. Intolerance on a large scale is incompatible with democracy because it will produce widespread conflict, as different groups try to impose their world views on each other. If disagreements are seen as treason or apostasy, then reasoned deliberation, which is at the core of good democratic practice, will no longer be possible and force will take over.

Finally, democracy requires its citizens to have a sense of political efficacy, that is, to believe that they can change things if they get involved in the political process. If politics is impervious to the needs of its citizens, either because the key institutions have been captured by unresponsive groups or because individuals are too apathetic to articulate their views, then democracy will wither. On the other hand, if people in general feel that they can change things by getting involved in politics this will encourage participation and democracy will prosper.

At the core of the modern democratic state is a relationship between the rulers and the ruled. There is essentially an 'invisible handshake' taking place in which citizens look to the state and to the government to protect and support them and, in exchange, they acknowledge they have obligations, such as paying their taxes, obeying the law and getting involved in the political process. Thus for democracy to work, its citizens need to have a combination of values and attitudes which are supportive of democratic politics. There needs to be a balance between citizen demands on the system for benefits and government assistance on the one hand, and a willingness to accept obligations to the state and to fellow citizens on the other. Tolerance, trust and efficacy are all different aspects of this balance since, without these, democracy is unlikely to work. If individuals are intolerant, mistrustful and lack a sense of efficacy they are unlikely to acknowledge their obligations to each other, while at the same time demanding that their needs are recognized above everyone else's needs.

This invisible handshake is a recurring theme and in the next section we outline the argument as it develops in the rest of this book.

Outline of the book

The early chapters of the book focus on mapping out the scope and breadth of civil society and the civic culture in Britain, as well as evaluating important changes that have occurred in them over the years. The starting point of the analysis in Chapter 2 is to examine the political values and attitudes of electors in Britain which underpin the civic culture. This involves looking at a number of different attitudes in the minds of the public, which are needed to make democracy work. These include tolerance of others; trust in the institutions of the state and in decision makers; efficacy, or the belief that political action by individuals and groups can change things; interest in politics or a willingness to pay attention to what is happening in the political system as a precursor to participating in the democratic process. These are all important aspects of democratic norms, but the most important question is the balance between the demands made by citizens on the state, on the one hand, and their willingness to accept obligations, on the other. So Chapter 2 examines that issue in detail, making the balance between rights and obligations a central concern.

Chapter 3 changes the focus from examining attitudes and values, to looking at political participation. There are debates about what constitutes political participation and we use data from a European wide survey conducted in 2002, which examines a variety of different types of participation in Britain, including voting, interest group activity, contacting decision makers and consumer participation. After mapping out the dimensions of political participation, the chapter then goes on to look at changes which have occurred over time. Such changes reveal a trend decline in most, though not all, forms of political participation in Britain. The central focus of the chapter is to explain why this trend decline has occurred, and we do this by looking closely at the most important form of participation from the point of view of the civic culture and governance, namely, voting. We briefly outline some of the important theories that have been used to explain electoral participation and then examine how two, which are particularly influential, cognitive engagement and general incentives theory, explain these trends. Both of these theories aim to provide a general account of the determinants of political participation from alternative but related perspectives.

After looking at norms, values and participation, Chapter 4 focuses the discussion closely on the most important institution of civil society, the political party. Parties play a key role in governance because they link citizens and political activists on the one hand with decision makers on the other. It turns out that the state of political parties in Britain plays a crucial role in explaining why political participation has been declining over time. The chapter begins by examining the role of political parties in our democracy and then moves on to explain why they are the most significant institutions of civil society. It examines political parties at three different levels of the political system; parties among the voters, parties among the voluntary activists; and finally, parties in Parliament. If parties are to work well then they need to operate effectively at each level of the political system. They need to have a loyal following in the electorate, enthusiastic support among the members and activists, and cohesive support in Parliament. The evidence shows that parties are weakening at all three levels, and so there is a paradox at the heart of government in Britain. This takes the form of a growing trend for governments to try to do more and more to influence the behaviour of the population, which runs alongside a depleting stock of political capital that can be drawn on to make governance effective and possible. This paradox is at the heart of the political weaknesses of British governments at the present time.

After focusing closely on one type of voluntary organization in Chapter 4, the subsequent chapter broadens the discussion to look at social capital and voluntary activity in Britain. Social capital has been a topic of some interest to a wide range of disciplines in recent years. It refers to a set of norms, values and practices in society which link citizens together in voluntary settings to help them to work together to solve common problems. It is important because it has been shown that if communities have high levels of social capital this brings with it many advantages, including better health, higher educational attainment, economic prosperity, improved life satisfaction, less crime and other benign effects. Thus it is very desirable for communities and countries to have social capital. However, the evidence in this chapter shows that social capital has been declining over time in Britain, and this is partly responsible for the weakening of the civic culture and also for a decline in the effectiveness of government, a topic we return to in a later chapter.

Chapter 6 looks at the media in Britain, a topic of considerable interest to observers of British politics. The media play a key role in informing citizens about the society they live in and also about the performance of governments which rule them. The media are a key conduit between the citizen and the state, providing news, comment, and analysis which helps citizens to make sense of the political world. The chapter begins by mapping out media usage in Britain, that is, newspaper consumption, television watching, radio listening and the use of the internet. Subsequently, the central focus of the chapter is an examination of how the media influences politics in Britain. The chapter shows that the media influences political attitudes and political participation and it does so via a number of mechanisms such as agenda setting and priming, and these are discussed in the chapter. Therefore, the media are important players in influencing the civic culture in Britain and, potentially, can influence all aspects of citizenship including norms, values, voluntary activity and participation, and most importantly voting behaviour. Understanding the media is very relevant for understanding how citizenship is created and maintained in the long run.

Chapter 7 returns to the theme of the balance between rights and obligations introduced in Chapter 2, but it does so from a comparative perspective. The central concern of the chapter is to compare and contrast Britain with other advanced industrial democracies to see how typical the country is in relation to political participation and various political attitudes. The advanced industrial countries looked at in the chapter are the thirty member states of the Organisation for Economic Co-operation and Development (OECD). The OECD consists of countries such as France, Germany, Spain, Canada and the United States, which are comparable in their economic and political development to Britain. The chapter concentrates on examining the growth of government across these industrial countries and explaining why this growth has occurred. What is undoubtedly true is that governments have grown in all of these countries over time, and Britain is no exception. It is a universal trend which reflects the fact that there is a strong demand for government intervention in the economy and in society in all contemporary democracies. The expansion of the franchise is a background factor which has contributed to this development, but the growth of the state has arisen ultimately because citizens want it. They value the protection from the risks and uncertainties of the private market at different stages of their lives, and they support social protection because it helps them to deal with these uncertainties. There are many market failures in the contemporary world and this is the origin of the demand for state intervention.

Chapter 8 changes the focus of analysis in comparison with the earlier chapters to look at the consequences of the civic culture rather than its characteristics and causes. It examines the extent to which civil society helps to make government effective, a topic which has been neglected in the literature on civic engagement. As in Chapter 7, a comparative approach is taken in order to understand the relationship between civil society and the effectiveness of the state in delivering the public policies that citizens want. It turns out that there is quite a strong relationship between a healthy civic culture and the delivery of effective policies, indicating that civil society plays a very important role in supporting good government. Towards the end of the chapter we examine the dynamics of government effectiveness in Britain in order to relate the decline of the civic culture charted earlier in the book with a weakening of the effectiveness of British government over time.

Chapter 9 rounds off the discussion by examining the question of what governments can do, if anything, to influence the trends identified in earlier chapters. The discussion is framed in relation to the 'Big Society' programme advocated by David Cameron, which calls for a resurgence of volunteering and local citizen activism in Britain. The chapter looks at the relationship between political centralization and the effectiveness of government, showing that the excessive centralization of the British state is damaging the effectiveness of the state in delivering the policies that people want. The Big Society programme is therefore welcome, but the chapter raises considerable doubts about its effectiveness, given the radical programme of cuts in government and in the welfare state planned by the coalition government at the time of writing. There is little evidence to support the idea that a retreat by government from the provision of public services will automatically give rise to a resurgence of volunteering at the local level, and in fact the evidence points in the opposite direction.

Overall, therefore, this book examines the characteristics, causes and consequences of civil society in Britain. As well as examining the scope of civic engagement in relation to values, norms and participation, it looks at the key factors which explain the trends we are observing both over time and in relation to the experience of other countries. The book highlights a malaise at the heart of civic culture in Britain today, linking this to more fundamental issues such as the rise in inequality and the decline of social capital. It is not an easy story to tell and it leads to the disturbing conclusion that one of the world's oldest democracies has a political system and a political culture which is increasingly not fit for purpose.

2

Changing Political Values and Attitudes

Why are political values, beliefs and attitudes important to democracy? The answer to this question is rooted in the relationship between the beliefs of citizens and the effectiveness of democratic government. In essence, for a democracy to work properly its citizens need to share certain basic values and beliefs. To elaborate on this point, a citizen might be highly critical of the government of the day and strongly prefer another party to be in power. But this feeling represents no challenge to democracy and in fact helps to sustain the democratic process by encouraging that citizen to become involved. On the other hand, if the same citizen is highly critical of the political system as a whole and holds key institutions such as Parliament, the Civil Service and the Judiciary in contempt, this is a different matter. If most citizens think that politicians are corrupt and in it for what they can get, and the institutions they serve irrelevant or venal, then they are likely to ignore politics altogether or try to undermine government processes. If these views are widespread in society then democracy will not function effectively. Thus the values and beliefs citizens have about their own political system and their role in it are crucial to the effectiveness of democratic politics.

This chapter is devoted to examining the political attitudes and beliefs which exist in contemporary Britain and their relationship to democratic practice. It looks at six key sets of attitudes which are important for a well functioning democracy to work:

1. citizen attitudes to the scope of government or the expectations of ordinary people about what government should deliver to its citizens;
2. views about citizen obligations to the state and the willingness of individuals to meet those obligations;
3. political tolerance or the willingness of citizens to acknowledge and accept differences of opinions;
4. trust in the institutions of the political system and in fellow citizens;
5. political efficacy or the feeling that getting involved in the political process can change things;
6. levels of interest in politics and public affairs.

These are all aspects of the civic culture or the values and beliefs held by ordinary citizens which sustain or undermine democracy.

What do citizens want from the state?

The first topic and in many ways the most important one in a democracy concerns the role of the state, or the extent to which UK citizens want the state to do things and intervene in their lives. Attitudes to the scope of government in Britain can be seen in Table 2.1, which looks at this by examining levels of support for different types of policies. The data come from the British respondents to the International Social Survey Programme Role of Government Survey, conducted in 2006. This was a comparative study of citizen attitudes to government policy making conducted in some thirty-two different countries. It included countries such as Australia, France, Germany, Japan, and the United States as well as Britain, and overall had more than 83,000 respondents. We examine only British respondents here, but will return to making international comparisons in Chapter 7.

A battery of question in the survey asked respondents to indicate the extent to which they thought that it was the government's responsibility to do various things. Table 2.1 shows that in Britain citizens gave a high priority to government support for healthcare, for old-age pensions and also for the protection of the environment. There was rather less enthusiasm for government support for students, for controls on prices, and for state investment in industry, although it is still true to say that substantial majorities of respondents were inclined to support such policies. Further down the list of priorities came policies to redistribute income from the rich to the poor and for the provision of affordable housing by the state. It would not be true to say that large majorities of citizens opposed such policies, but positive support for them was significantly less than for healthcare and pensions. Finally, at the bottom of the list there was relatively meagre support for state job creation and for boosting income support for the unemployed.

To some extent these views are in accord with existing priorities for public spending, since health and pensions are much bigger items in the national budget that financial support for students and investment in industry. Also there is a clear distinction that people make between those considered to be deserving of support such as the retired and elderly, and those considered to be a lesser priority, such as the unemployed.

Table 2.1   Views about the role of government in Britain in 2006

	Definitely should not (%)	Probably should not (%)	Probably should (%)	Definitely should (%)
Provide healthcare for the sick	0	1	28	71
Provide a decent living standard for the elderly	0	3	37	60
Impose strict laws to protect the environment	1	7	44	48
Provide financial help to students	2	9	55	34
Keep prices under control	4	12	52	32
Help industry to grow	2	11	58	29
Reduce income differences between rich and poor	10	23	40	27
Provide affordable housing	3	11	60	25
Provide a job for everyone who wants one	15	30	39	17
Provide a decent living standard for the unemployed	12	33	43	12

Source: ISSP, *Role of Government Survey* 2006, (N=930).

Table 2.2 examines a different aspect of the same question, this time by asking people about their priorities for public spending. Once again healthcare and pensions are at the top of the list, while education, which did not appear in Table 2.1, is a close third. The public were rather less enthusiastic about spending on the police, law and order and the environment in comparison with the big welfare spending programmes, although clear majorities thought that government should probably or definitely spend more on these areas. There was much less enthusiasm for spending on defence, unemployment benefits, and above all, on culture and the arts. The latter is a bit of a Cinderella in the minds of the public.

The government plays a key role in supporting and developing the economy, and this was never more apparent than during the bail-out of the banking system following the 2008 financial crisis. The public's

Table 2.2   Spending priorities of British citizens in 2006

	Spend much less (%)	Spend less (%)	Spend the same (%)	Spend more (%)	Spend much more (%)
Health	0	1	17	54	27
Old-age pensions	0	2	26	48	24
Education	0	1	27	51	22
The police and law enforcement	1	2	36	45	16
The environment	1	3	40	43	13
Defence	7	18	46	21	9
Unemployment benefits	10	31	45	11	3
Culture and the arts	17	30	43	9	2

Source: ISSP, *Role of Government Survey* 2006, (N=930).

views about government spending on different aspects of economic policy can be seen in Table 2.3. The table shows that there was strong support for government intervention to create new products and new jobs in industry, but rather less enthusiasm for propping up declining industries in order to save jobs. There was little enthusiasm for deregulation as a means of stimulating economic growth, and even less support for cuts in public spending as a means of stimulating the economy. The public have a broadly Keynesian view of the role of government in economic management. However, this has its limits since there was very limited support for the idea of reducing the working week in order to create jobs. Overall, the public see the state as having an important role in the development of the economy and in job creation, but they are not persuaded that the way to do this is by de-regulation and cuts in government spending.

It is clear that British citizens expect quite a lot from their governments. They see support for citizens in sickness and in old age, and investment in the next generation in the form of educational spending as being absolutely central to the role of the state. They are also generally supportive of government intervention in the economy for the purpose of developing new technologies and new jobs. There is little evidence to suggest that citizens support a slimmed-down state which

Table 2.3   Public attitudes to government intervention in the economy in 2006

	Strongly against (%)	Against (%)	Neither (%)	Favour (%)	Strongly favour (%)
Support for industry to develop new products	0	1	12	59	27
Financing projects to create new jobs	1	5	18	53	23
Support declining industries to protect jobs	3	15	23	47	14
Less government regulation of industry	3	9	43	33	12
Cuts in government spending	8	24	31	27	11
Reduce the working week to create new jobs	8	27	35	23	7

Source: ISSP, *Role of Government Survey* 2006 (N=930).

would provide law and order and defence of the realm, but abandon the big welfare programmes which support large numbers of people.

However citizens also perceive the limits of government. There is scepticism about whether or not the state should try to provide jobs for everyone, and much less enthusiasm about supporting the unemployed in comparison with the retired. Table 2.2 is particularly revealing in this respect, since it is apparent that the public would be quite happy to see government drastically reduce support for the arts, and although they do not think this about defence, there is little enthusiasm for increasing spending in that area.

What of the other side of the coin? Namely the willingness of citizens to meet their obligations to support the state and to provide the resources for public spending. We examine this question next.

What do citizens think they owe the state?

We can examine public attitudes to the obligations of being a citizen using another survey conducted in 2004 as part of the International Social Survey Programme. This was the Citizenship Survey conducted in a total of 37 countries with an overall sample of more than 52,000 respondents. A set of questions in the survey probed what respondents thought it takes to be a good citizen. Responses to this battery provide considerable insight into the sense of obligations that individuals have towards their fellow citizens.

Again Table 2.4 contains data for British respondents only, and it can be seen that there are large variations in the priorities that individuals attach to the various duties and obligations of citizenship. It is perhaps reassuring from the point of view of society in general that there are very strong norms supporting the idea that people should obey the law and also that they should pay their taxes. In many ways these are the two central obligations that all citizens should have in the modern state, the first to maintain public order and the second to maintain public spending. There is also a strong norm that people should vote in elections, although this was not as strong as the other two.

In addition, there were also reasonably strong norms that people should try to understand different points of view when it comes to dealing with other people, with more than three-quarters of the respondents thinking this is important or very important. This norm of tolerance for other points of view is essential to an effective democracy, as the earlier discussion indicated. There is also a surprisingly strong norm that citizens should be willing to ensure that the government was accountable, in the sense of keeping an eye on what it is doing. On the other hand, there is rather less support for the idea that people should try to help others who are less well off than themselves, and in this respect respondents made a clear distinction between helping their fellow citizens and helping the citizens of other countries. They are significantly more enthusiastic about the former than the latter.

Towards the foot of Table 2.4 are the low priority obligations that citizens acknowledged. Some respondents felt that it is a citizen's duty to buy products for ethical, environmental or political reasons, but many do not share this view. Similarly, the view that it is a citizen's duty to do voluntary work is very much a minority opinion, not widely held in Britain. Table 2.4 confirms that there are strong norms in our society supporting the citizen's sense of obligations to the state and to the wider society. It is not true that most people want something for nothing, in the sense that they demand benefits from the state without being willing to acknowledge their obligations. In that sense the data is reassuring. On the other hand the table shows that there are minorities, and in some cases significant minorities who do not acknowledge these obligations. Some people did not think it is important that the good citizen should pay their taxes or vote in elections, so there are some who demand ben-

Table 2.4   Perceptions of the good citizen in Britain in 2004

	Not at all important (%)	Not important (%)	Not sure (%)	Important (%)	Very important (%)
Always obey the law	1	1	3	26	69
Never evade taxes	2	3	3	24	67
Always vote in elections	8	10	14	28	40
Understand others' opinions	2	5	13	44	36
Keep watch on government	5	9	18	39	29
Help the less privileged in Britain	2	12	17	46	24
Serve in the military	14	17	15	33	22
Help the less privileged abroad	5	21	19	39	17
Buy products to support the environment	11	19	23	36	12
Be active in a voluntary association	21	30	23	24	4

Note: The responses in the table have been recoded from a 7-point scale to a 5-point scale by combining 2 and 3 to make 'Not important' and 5 and 6 to make 'Important'.

Source: ISSP, *Citizenship Survey*, 2004 (N=833).

efits without acknowledging obligations. An earlier analysis of rather similar data showed that this group tends to be people at the bottom of the socio-economic scale (Pattie, Seyd and Whiteley, 2004). Thus those people with the least stake in the system in the sense of being the poorest, least educated and most likely to be unemployed were the least likely to acknowledge their obligations as citizens. Fortunately such attitudes are confined to a relatively small minority.

We see in Table 2.4 that there was a strong norm that people should pay their taxes, and Table 2.5 probes attitudes to this all-important obligation in more detail. This table gives insight into how respondents view the fairness of the tax system in practice. Respondents were asked to comment on the fairness of current taxation for high-income, middle-income and low-income individuals. It can be seen that opinions are

Table 2.5   Attitudes to taxation in Britain in 2006

Taxes for	Much too low (%)	Too low (%)	About right (%)	Too high (%)	Much too high (%)
High-income groups	4	26	41	19	10
Middle-income groups	0	3	50	37	10
Low-income groups	0	2	30	44	24

Source: ISSP, *Role of Government Survey* 2006 (N=930).

fairly balanced over the fairness of current levels of taxation for high-income individuals. Many people feel that this group should be paying more taxes. However, the same point cannot be made about middle-income and low-income individuals. In the case of middle-income groups the most popular response was to say that tax levels were 'about right', although significantly more respondents thought that taxes were too high rather than too low. However, in the case of low income individuals there is a clear consensus that taxation levels are too high, a view taken by two-thirds of respondents. This data suggests that while people think that citizens should pay their taxes, there is also a feeling that affluent members of the community are getting a much better deal than the less affluent. While it is not true that everyone wants taxes to be reduced, nonetheless British citizens perceive a distinct imbalance in the tax obligations of different people in the community.

Are people tolerant?

Moving on to the issue of tolerance, we saw in Table 2.4 that Britons thought that it is very important to understand different points of view in our society. However, this is a relatively easy test of tolerance, which few people are likely to disagree with. A much more stringent test is to ask about tolerance of unpopular groups such as religious extremists or racists. When individuals are being asked to tolerate people that are widely disliked their answers may be different. There are a set of questions in the Citizenship Survey which asked about the respondent's willingness to allow unpopular groups to hold public meetings. The three groups cited were religious extremists, individuals who want to overthrow the government by force, and racists.

The responses to these questions are revealing, with Britons showing a fair degree of intolerance. The greatest intolerance was shown towards people who want to overthrow the elected government, with more than eight out of ten thinking that such people should probably or definitely not be allowed to hold public meetings. This may be tapping into to public concerns about political terrorism. About three-quarters of respondents thought the same thing about racists. Finally, the most tolerance was shown towards religious extremists, except even in this case about two-thirds of respondents thought that they should not be allowed to hold meetings. Thus it is evident that most Britons are not very tolerant of unpopular minorities. In fairness, the common characteristic of these groups is that they are likely to be very intolerant themselves, and so part of the public's reaction to them may arise from this fact. But it is evident that respondents recognize quite strict limits on freedom of speech.

Another approach to measuring tolerance is to ask individuals how important it is for government to protect the rights of minorities. In effect, this is a measure of the priority individuals attach to protecting the rights of people who are likely to be different from themselves. The Citizenship Survey asked respondents to indicate how much importance they attached to governments respecting the rights of minorities. The data shows that there is a strong norm supporting the idea that government should do this, with some 44 per cent attaching the highest priority to it, and only about 1 per cent the lowest priority. Clearly, while tolerance for unpopular groups was limited, there is nonetheless a strong feeling that the rights of minorities should be protected. Norms of tolerance in Britain are strong enough to recognize and support a diversity of opinions.

Do people trust their fellow citizens and the state?

Another important factor which supports democratic government relates to the extent to which individuals trust the government and their fellow citizens. Recent research has emphasized the importance of trust between people in sustaining an effective democracy. In the literature on social capital introduced in Chapter 1, interpersonal trust plays a big role in defining this concept. One prominent theorist, Robert Putnam, defines social capital as 'features of social organization, such as trust, norms and networks that can improve the efficiency of society by facilitating co-ordinated actions' (1993: 167). The argument is that high levels of interpersonal trust in society are a powerful indicator of high levels of social capital and, as we pointed out in Chapter 1, this appears to have many benign consequences such as reducing crime, improving health, enhancing educational performance and stimulating economic prosperity (Putnam, 2000). We will discuss this issue more fully in Chapter 5, but for now it is interesting to examine trust in broad terms.

The Citizenship Survey showed that Britons were more or less equally divided on the merits of trusting other people. A small majority of British respondents erred on the side of caution saying that they had to be careful when dealing with other people when responding to the question rather than saying that they trusted other people. In fact Britons were just above the average in their willingness to trust others in comparison with the citizens of the other thirty-six countries in the Citizenship Survey.

When asked about their willingness to trust their own government, there was a clear tendency for people to be less trusting than when they were asked about trusting fellow citizens. Approximately 40 per cent disagreed or strongly disagreed that people in government can be trusted, with only 28 per cent agreeing or strongly agreeing with the proposition. The sceptics outweighed their counterparts by a significant margin. The lack of trust in government is debilitating to effective state action, since governments spend a lot of time trying to persuade people to do things, and trust is an essential requirement if such persuasion is to be effective. On the other hand it is important not to overstate this, since citizens need to keep governments accountable, and so a certain amount of distrust of government is probably a good thing in a democracy.

Do citizens feel they can change circumstances ?

The fifth aspect of beliefs and attitudes relates to political efficacy, or the feeling that individuals can change the state of affairs if they get involved in politics. Efficacy plays a very important role in motivating people to participate since without it much of participation becomes a mere ritual; if ordinary citizens believe that their actions will change things for the better then this creates an incentive for them to get involved and in turn this will contribute to the effectiveness of government and democracy.

The Citizenship Survey contained a number of indicators of efficacy, two of which are particularly revealing. Individuals were asked if they agreed or disagreed with the statement: 'People like me don't have any say about what government does'. A surprising 54 per cent of respondents agreed or strongly agreed with the statement, and only 26 per cent disagreed or strongly disagreed. Thus individuals who feel a sense of efficacy in Britain are in a clear minority. The other statement asked people: 'How likely is it that you would be able to do something about an unjust law?' Revealingly, some 61 per cent thought that it was not very likely or not at all likely that they could do anything, with only 13 per cent thinking that it was very likely that they could. Once more, there is a great deal of scepticism among Britons about their ability to change the policies of their government. This evidence suggests that feelings of efficacy in the British political system are not high. Most people do not think that they can change the situation or that Parliament is responsive to their concerns.

How interested are people in politics?

The final topic we examine in this discussion of the attitudes and beliefs is the level of interest in politics. An effective democracy does not require its citizens to be constantly monitoring politics or to take a strong interest in all aspects of policy making and government. But if very few people take such an interest then democratic accountability is unlikely to work properly. In this situation governments will be able to take actions that are contrary to the wishes of most people without being much concerned about a citizen backlash.

The survey asked a simple question: 'How interested would you say you personally are in politics?' In response to this question about two-thirds said they were at least somewhat interested in politics and about 40 per cent said they were fairly or very interested. Respondents who declared that they were not interested at all made up only 10 per cent of the population. This suggests that Britons in general are attentive enough to the political process for government to be held accountable.

We have reviewed six different aspects of people's attitudes and beliefs about the working of democracy in Britain. As we have seen, citizens make significant demands on the state and their expectations are high that it will provide services such as healthcare and education. At the same time, they have strong norms supportive of obeying the law and paying taxes, and thus there is little evidence of a major imbalance between their demand for services and the recognition that they have obligations to pay for these. With regard to tolerance, trust and efficacy, however, there are clear limits to the norms which support democracy. Britons are aware that it is important to take into account differing views, but they are not very tolerant of giving a platform to unpopular minorities. Similarly, opinions are divided about the value of trusting others and there is a clear preference for not trusting the government. Equally, British citizens do not have a strong sense of efficacy, since most do not believe that they can change matters by political action or that Parliament is responsive to their concerns. On the other hand, most people take at least some interest in politics and this helps to keep democratic politics accountable.

The data up to this point provides a snapshot of opinions in Britain in the early part of the twenty-first century. But have opinions changed over time? We examine this issue next.

Changes in norms and attitudes over time

The analysis in this chapter has used two different surveys to look at attitudes and norms in Britain, both conducted by the International Social Survey Programme. The Role of Government Survey has been carried out four times, in 1985, 1990, 1996 and 2006, with many of the same indicators, so we can use it to examine trends in attitudes over a period of more than twenty years. Unfortunately, the Citizenship Survey has only been conducted once, in 2004, and so it is not possible to track attitudes from that survey. This restricts our ability to monitor changes in citizen's sense of their obligations to the state over time. However, we can pick up one indicator of obligations, namely attitudes to taxation, from the Role of Government Survey and this will be discussed below.

In this section we will replicate as far as possible the responses examined in earlier tables but this time with a focus on changes in attitudes over time. We begin by examining changes in perceptions of government responsibilities in Table 2.6, which includes the percentage of respondents who said that the government should definitely be responsible for the provisions mentioned. It is noteworthy that the two most popular government responsibilities in Table 2.1, healthcare and pensions, remained top priorities over the twenty-one year period. What is also apparent, however, is that the percentage of support for them has declined between 1985 and 2006. Britons have clearly become more conservative about government support over time.

A similar pattern can be found in all of the other government responsibilities in the list, with some of the changes being quite dramatic. Thus

Table 2.6   Changes in perceptions of government responsibility, 1985 to 2006

Government definitely should do the following:	1985 (%)	1990 (%)	1996 (%)	2006 (%)
Provide healthcare for the sick	86	85	82	71
Provide a decent living standard for the old	79	78	71	60
Impose strict laws to protect the environment	—	—	62	48
Provide financial help to students	—	49	37	34
Keep prices under control	61	49	42	32
Help industry to grow	54	43	40	29
Reduce income differences between rich and poor	48	42	35	27
Provide affordable housing	—	—	62	48
Provide a job for everyone who wants one	38	24	28	17
Provide a decent living standard for the unemployed	45	32	28	11

Note: Dashes indicate missing data in those years.

Source: ISSP, *Role of Government Surveys* 1985–2006.

the percentage of respondents who think that the government should control prices has halved, as has the percentage who think that the government should create jobs. Support for the unemployed fell even more dramatically, and there was also a significant decline in support for government house building, even though this particular indicator was measured only over a ten-year period. In that case it might in part reflect the fact that social housing is now largely the responsibility of third-sector bodies such as housing associations. Equally, the environment as a priority appears to have declined, as has support for government investment in industry and financial aid for students. The overall pattern of answers suggests that the British public are losing their enthusiasm for government intervention right across the board, although support still remains high for the core activities of health and pensions.

Table 2.7 shows the changes in spending priorities over the period. The table identifies the proportions who say that government should spend more on the activities described earlier in Table 2.2. In this case

Table 2.7   Changes in spending priorities, 1985 to 2006

Government should spend more on:	1985 (%)	1990 (%)	1996 (%)	2006 (%)
Health	87	88	90	78
Old-age pensions	73	80	76	69
Education	72	77	82	69
The police and law enforcement	38	48	70	58
The environment	34	59	41	53
Defence	17	8	17	28
Unemployment benefits	40	35	33	13
Culture and the arts	9	12	6	10

Source: ISSP, *Role of Government Surveys* 1985–2006.

the pattern of responses is more mixed in comparison with Table 2.6. It appears that support for spending on health, pensions and education fell, but only by relatively modest amounts. In contrast, support for spending on the police, the environment and defence all rose. This is consistent with the changing issue agenda in British politics over this ten-year period. Research has shown that the British public became much more pre-occupied with issues of personal security and safety in the mid-2000s in comparison with the mid-1990s (Clarke, Sanders, Stewart and Whiteley, 2009: 57). This would account for the increase in spending priorities for the police and the armed forces.

Finally, while there was little change in the low priority attached to spending on the arts and culture, there was a dramatic fall in support for spending on the unemployed. It is important to note that the years between 1996 and 2006 were a period of rising prosperity and economic growth. It seems plausible that sympathy for the unemployed was coloured by this experience, and the feeling that everyone can get a job if they really want one during a period of prosperity.

Table 2.8 shows changes in the responses to the indicators of attitudes to government economic policies described in Table 2.3. It contains the percentages of respondents who favour the policies described. Once again we see a pattern of declining support with a couple of exceptions. There was a modest decline in government support for industry to develop new products and a rather bigger decline in support for financ-

Table 2.8   Changes in attitudes to government economic policies, 1985 to 2006

Policies	1985 (%)	1990 (%)	1996 (%)	2006 (%)
Support for industry to develop new products	89	88	86	81
Financing projects to create new jobs	86	82	84	72
Support declining industries to protect jobs	49	59	62	56
Less government regulation of industry	53	42	40	40
Cuts in government spending	37	41	43	35
Reduce the working week to create new jobs	49	41	37	28

Source: ISSP, *Role of Government Surveys* 1985–2006.

ing job-creation schemes. However, sympathy for government support for declining industries rose during this period, although it still remains a less popular activity than some others in the list. There was a clear decline in support for de-regulation, while enthusiasm for cuts in government spending did not change and remained at a fairly low level. Finally, reductions in the working week as a means of job creation became even more unpopular over time.

Table 2.9 looks at changes in attitudes to taxation and so picks up on the data in Table 2.5. The comparison is over ten years, since the question was not asked earlier. The striking finding from this table is the growth in the perception that taxes on middle-income groups are too high. There was a modest increase in the number of people who thought that taxes on the high-income groups were excessive and an even more modest reduction in the numbers who thought that taxes on low-income groups are too high. But it appears that there is something of a middle-income taxpayer revolt at work. Taxation has never been very popular but it is appears to be increasingly unpopular for the middle-income groups.

Overall, these tables tell a different story from the cross-sectional analysis of the 2006 data discussed earlier. There is fairly clear evidence that over a period of years the UK population has grown more conservative in feeling that government should do less and should take less money from the average citizen in the form of taxation. There are some exceptions to this trend, such as the desire to spend more on policing and defence but, those aside, social attitudes appear to be trending

Table 2.9   Changes in attitudes to taxation, 1996 to 2006

Taxes are too high for:	1996 (%)	2006 (%)
High-income groups	17	26
Middle-income groups	30	43
Low-income groups	69	62

Source: ISSP, *Role of Government Surveys* 1985–2006.

towards a desire to see a less intrusive government which does less and spends less.

We mentioned earlier that it is not possible to track indicators from the Citizenship Survey over time, but there is one measure in the Role of Government Surveys which relates to the question of obeying the law. Table 2.4 showed that the norms supporting law abiding behaviour in Britain are very strong. But have they changed over time? The Role of Government Surveys asked respondents the following question in 1985 and then again in 2006:

> In general, would you say that people should obey the law without exception, or are there exceptional occasions on which people should follow their consciences even if it means breaking the law?

There was very little change in the responses to this question over the twenty-one year period. A majority of respondents thought that people should follow their consciences on occasions in 1985 and a similar majority thought the same thing in 2006. This suggests that the norms on obeying the law have not changed very much over this period. Clearly, if the citizen's sense of obligation has not really changed, this cannot be the explanation of why people appear to want less government. So what explains the fall in the demand for government?

The decline in the demand for government

One possible explanation for the decline in the demand for government is widespread citizen dissatisfaction with the performance of government in delivering the key services and policies referred to in Table 2.6. If people increasingly believe that government does not deliver, then it

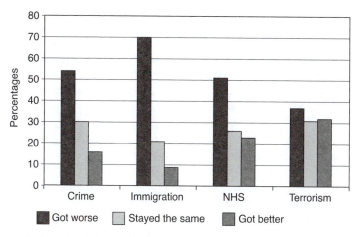

Source: Continuous Monitoring Survey of the British Election Study (N=94,943).

Figure 2.1   Perceptions of policy delivery, 2004 to 2010

is not surprising that they think government should do less. Evidence supporting this hypothesis can be seen in Figure 2.1 which uses data from the Continuous Monitoring Survey of the British Election Study, which is a series of monthly surveys of the electorate starting in 2004 and continuing up to the present time (see http://bes2009-10.org). When the responses to these surveys are averaged over time they can be used to determine if citizens think that policy delivery by government is improving, remaining unchanged, or getting worse. The figure shows that in four key areas more citizens in Britain thought that delivery had got worse than thought the opposite. This was particularly true for immigration but it was also true of the National Health Service, despite the fact that the Labour government had increased spending on the NHS by a large amount during this period.

Figure 2.1 shows that, generally, British citizens think that government is failing to deliver on key policy areas. It can of course be argued that these data merely reflect the relative unpopularity of the Labour government, particularly during its final term of office from 2005 to 2010. But in the same surveys, questions were asked about the performance of a hypothetical Conservative government. Respondents were invited to pass judgement on its performance in the same four areas of policy. In the event, the replies were not that much different from those in Figure 2.1. Individuals who thought that a Conservative government would do worse outnumbered those who thought it would do better, both in relation to immigration and the National Health Service. Responses were about evenly balanced on crime, and slightly more optimistic than pessimistic on anti-terrorism policies. There may be some support for the argument that perceptions of policy failure in Figure 2.1 is due to an anti-Labour bias, but this is far from being the whole explanation. It is apparent that many people in Britain believe that governments – all governments – are not very good at delivering. Not surprisingly these views make it less likely that the public will think that government should spend more and try to do more.

There is a second factor which might help to explain the growing conservatism of the public in relation to policy delivery. This is the belief that the forces of globalization are increasingly making it difficult for British governments to be masters in their own house. The point here is that if voters think that the British government is less able to deliver on policies because it is increasingly constrained by the outside world, particularly the European Union, then they are less likely to support policies which call for additional taxation and spending.

The evidence to support this idea again comes from the Continuous Monitoring Survey of the British Election Study. Respondents were asked in each of the surveys which government they thought was most influential in determining the state of the national economy, the British Government or the European Union. In the first survey in April 2004 some 43 per cent thought that the British government had most influence, 14 per cent thought it was the European Union and 37 per cent thought it was both equally. By December 2010 this had changed, with 38 per cent thinking that it was the British government, 20 per cent choosing the European Union, and again 37 per cent thinking it was both equally. Thus a relatively small but discernable shift in attributions of responsibility for the state of the British economy occurred over time, with fewer people thinking that the British government exerts most influence.

Conclusion

This analysis shows that British political culture is fairly healthy since the demand for government policy interventions are generally supported by norms, which hold that people should obey the law and pay their taxes. However, the trends suggest that Britons are gradually moving away from the belief that the state should provide health, welfare and education, and moreover, they increasingly appear to resent the burden of taxation on middle England.

It is important not to exaggerate these trends since there is still very strong support for government provision of the basic services which make up the welfare state. But people are less supportive of big government and the evidence in Table 2.6 is particularly instructive – they increasingly expect to support the burdens of old age and sickness themselves, and are less inclined to see government as the sole provider in these areas. The very large reductions in support for job creation, unemployment benefits and the provision of affordable housing, together with the drop in support for redistribution suggest that people are less inclined to turn to government to solve their problems. In this respect the role of government is being weakened.

Moreover, there is evidence to suggest that this is happening because of a combination of public scepticism about policy performance, and also about the ability of governments to deliver in a world in which much contemporary policy making takes place at the European level. This chapter has focused on norms and attitudes, but what about behaviour? Government needs to be supported by the active involvement of its citizens as well as by their beliefs. We examine this issue in the next chapter.

3

Trends in Participation in Britain

Political participation is at the heart of democratic government and civil society, and without it there can be no effective democracy. Participation refers to activities such as, voting, lobbying politicians, attending political meetings, joining protest rallies and being active in political parties. These activities have a common thread involving volunteering as, for ordinary citizens, they are unpaid, but they are all designed to directly or indirectly influence the policies and/or personnel of the state. Of course attempts by individuals to influence decision making may be very parochial, for example, a citizen may attend her MP's surgery in order to get advice about claiming benefits. But they might also be quite general, when the same citizen joins a protest march to try to change British foreign policy.

One interesting feature is that with the single exception of voting, political participation engages only a minority of citizens, and some types of participation involve quite small minorities. Figure 3.1 shows eleven different types of participation undertaken by Britons in 2002, measured using data from the European Social Survey of that year. It can be seen that the most popular was voting followed by signing a petition and then consumer participation, that is, buying or boycotting products for political or ethical reasons. In fact, petition signing and consumer participation often go together since campaigning organizations frequently set up their stalls in shopping centres, hoping to get passers-by to sign up to their campaigns. The reason why there is so much petition signing is that petitions range over a wide variety of issues, taking in local concerns such as planning decisions, to regional questions, for example, the expansion of London's airports, and to national concerns such as the war in Iraq.

The two types of consumer participation have now become known as boycotting and buycotting and, as we shall see below, these have grown in popularity in recent years. One of the reasons for this is that consumer participation is very easy to do, since anyone who shops in a local supermarket or grocery store can become involved. Many people buy fair-trade coffee for example, or boycott products because they believe animal cruelty was involved in their manufacture. The citizen can do this fairly easily in the course of their everyday lives.

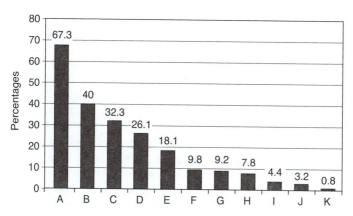

Note: The question asked was have respondents carried out the following political activities over the previous year:

A: Voted in the 2001 General Election?
B: Signed a petition?
C: Bought products for political, ethical or environmental reasons?
D: Boycotted products for political, ethical or environmental reasons?
E: Contacted a politician or government official?
F: Worn or displayed a campaign badge or sticker?
G: Worked in a voluntary organization or association?
H: Donated money to a political organization?
I: Taken part in a lawful public demonstration?
J: Worked in a political party or action group?
K: Participated in an illegal protest activity?

Source: European Social Survey, 2002; see http://www.europeansocialsurvey.org/.

Figure 3.1   Types of participation in Britain

After consumer participation the next most popular activity is contacting a politician or public official. This very often involves a personal matter, such as asking officials for help in navigating the labyrinthine welfare benefits system, but it can also involve citizens lobbying their MP about some general aspect of government policy. After this, the fifth most popular activity is wearing or displaying a campaign sticker or badge, something that would have been boosted in 2002 by the general election of the previous year. This is a form of campaigning, and one step up from it involves joining a protest demonstration. Protesting involved less than one in twenty citizens in 2002, and a further step up from that involves taking part in an illegal protest, for example, animal rights protesters breaking into research laboratories, and demonstrators occupying construction sites to prevent road building. The latter involved less than one per cent of the population in 2002, which is a small number in relative terms but quite a large number in absolute terms.

Each step in this hierarchy of campaigning involves a steep rise in the costs, with protesting being more costly than wearing a campaign badge, and illegal protesting being very high cost since it carries the risk of prosecution. This helps to explain why few people carry out the very high cost activities and many more, the low cost ones. Just short of 10 per cent of the population reported working in a voluntary organization in 2002, and only 3 per cent worked in a political party, a figure which was probably boosted by the general election of 2001. Given the importance of political parties to democracy, this is a very small section of the population and, as we shall see below, this proportion has been declining over time.

The forms of participation described in Figure 3.1 involve trying to influence elected representatives or public officials, but in addition there is an extra dimension to participation involving citizens directly attempting to influence the provision of the public services they use on a day-to-day basis. If a parent seeks to change the delivery of education in their child's school, or an NHS patient tries to change the way their local hospital provides treatment, they are clearly trying to influence agents of the state, namely teachers and doctors. This may be described as micro-participation and, in the past, has often not been recognized as a type of political participation. But since it involves changing the delivery of public services, albeit at a very local level, it nonetheless constitutes an important form of political participation (see Pattie, Seyd and Whiteley, 2004). Individuals are dealing with what one researcher calls 'street level bureaucrats' (Lipsky, 1980) and since this is the level at which most people have direct contact with the state, it becomes important for the political system.

Equally, there are informal types of participation such as people discussing politics in the pub, in the home or in the workplace. This can be important in elections as word-of-mouth communication is often more effective than media campaigning. In addition, there are 'sporadic interventionists' (Dowse and Hughes, 1977), that is, individuals who get involved in politics in response to local events, such as lobbying against a plan to build an incinerator in their area or to campaign in favour of a by-pass for their town. These forms of political participation are quite important but the participants often do not see themselves engaged in political participation, regarding what they are doing as a form of voluntary activity. We will return to a discussion of the relationship between voluntary activity and political participation in Chapter 5.

Changes in participation over time

There have been significant changes in political participation in Britain over time. This is most easily seen in the case of voting, which is the most important and visible form of political participation. Turnouts in successive general elections from 1945 to 2010 appear in Figure 3.2, and it is fairly clear that there has been a long-term trend decline in electoral participation over this period, subject to fluctuations, between successive elections. The high point of post-war turnouts occurred in 1950 which was the first, fully peace-time election after the Second World War. Almost nine out of ten eligible citizens voted in the 1950 election, but by 2010 it was just over six out of ten. In fact, Figure 3.2 probably gives an inaccurate measure of turnout over this period, since it is calculated as the ratio of people who voted to those on the electoral register. If individuals are not on the register, this will disqualify them from voting even if they wished to do so. If, for example, people move house in the year of a general election, they will still be eligible to vote at their old address, but not at the new one if the election occurs between the annual compilations of the register. This fact may very well discourage them from voting, leading to an underestimate of the number of people who could vote. On the other hand, if the same number of people vote but the register included the names of people who are currently missing from it, that would overestimate turnout. These problems with the electoral register have always been present and so they are unlikely to change the picture of electoral decline seen in Figure 3.2. Unless the

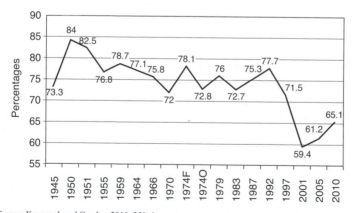

Source: Kavanagh and Cowley, 2010: 350–1.

Figure 3.2   Turnouts in general elections, 1945–2010.

accuracy of the register has increased or decreased over time, and there is no evidence of this, the problem will affect all eighteen general elections since the Second World War.

Figure 3.2 shows that since the high point of turnout in that first postwar election, electoral participation declined gradually during the 1950s and 1960s, but with the odd rally in the early 1970s and 1990s. However, the trend was remorselessly down with the decline accelerating dramatically after 1997. The low point of turnout was in 2001 and it increased only slightly in 2005 and then again in 2010. It is also true that low turnouts have been a feature of recent elections to the European Parliament, to the Scottish, Welsh and London assemblies, as well as the London mayoral elections. Overall, electoral participation in Britain has declined quite significantly since its heyday in the 1950s.

Electoral participation is easy to track because official turnout figures are provided after every election. Analysing other forms of participation is not so easy, either because there are no official figures, or because the survey evidence is patchy. However, a large-scale study of participation was conducted in Britain in 1984 by a team of researchers based at the University of Manchester (see Parry, Moyser and Day, 1992). It is possible to compare their findings with those from the European Social Survey in Figure 3.1. Differences in question wording and the measurement of variables mean that the comparisons between the two surveys are not exact, but they are reasonably accurate.

Figure 3.3 compares different types of participation almost twenty years apart, but it shows markedly that, in every case but one, participation has either declined or remained stable. Figure 3.3 confirms the earlier point that fewer people reported voting in a general election in 2002 than in 1984. In both cases the general election took place a year before the survey, so it provides a reasonably accurate picture of what happened. If we examine other forms of participation, many people reported signing a petition in the later survey, but it was many fewer than in 1984. Similarly, contacting politicians or public officials was well down. The decline in the number of people who worked in a political party is particularly noticeable, although there was a lesser decline in the numbers who worked for a voluntary organization. Similarly, the number of people who went on a protest march was down but in this case by a relatively small amount. The clear exception to this overall pattern relates to consumer participation with a large increase in the numbers of people boycotting products.

The growth of boycotting and buycotting has taken place as a consequence of increasing affluence and the rise of consumerism. If the

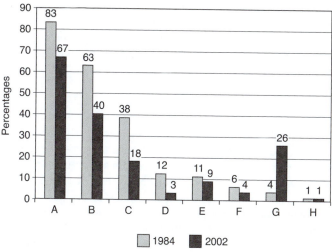

Note:
A: Voted in a general election;
B: Signed a petition;
C: Contacted a politician or government official;
D: Worked in a political party;
E: Worked in an organized group;
F: Taken part in a protest march or public demonstration;
G: Boycotted products for political, ethical or environmental reasons;
H: Participated in an illegal protest activity.

Source: Parry, Moyser and Day, 1992: 44; European Social Survey, 2002;
see http://www.europeansocialsurvey.org/.

Figure 3.3   Changes in participation, 1984–2002

market offers a growing array of choices of consumer goods, then it is
perhaps not surprising that many people apply ethical or political tests
to their purchases. However, as the earlier discussion indicates, the consumer culture is in some ways antithetical to a citizenship culture, since
it involves a market relationship. The good citizen should participate
regardless of the cash nexus, and so there is a question mark about the
extent to which a rise of consumerist forms of participation represents
an improvement in citizenship.

Given these trends, the obvious question is: why have they occurred?
It is most easy to address this in relation to voting because there is a
rich store of data focusing on electoral participation which goes back
to the 1960s. In the rest of this chapter, therefore, we will focus primarily

on electoral participation, although many of the points made about voting also apply to other forms of participation as well. We begin the discussion by looking at who votes and who does not vote before considering what might explain the trends observed in Figure 3.2.

Who votes?

Table 3.1 shows the demographic characteristics of voters and non-voters at the time of the 2005 general election. The first thing to notice about the table is the sharp differences in turnout between age groups. Only 43 per cent of the youngest group, aged 18 to 25, voted in that election, which means that close to six out of ten did not. This is in sharp contrast to the 83 per cent turnout among those aged 56 to 65 and the 82 per cent of those who voted over the age of 65 years. There is clearly a huge difference between successive generations of citizens in their voting behaviour. It has always been true that younger cohorts are less likely to vote than older groups, but the gap between the young and the old has grown much larger in recent years (Clarke, Sanders, Stewart and Whiteley, 2004).

Table 3.1 also shows that there is something of a 'gender' gap in electoral participation, with women more likely to vote than men, and a 'sector' gap with public sector workers more likely to vote than workers in the private sector. Not surprisingly, ethnic minority groups are significantly less likely to vote than the ethnic majority. The relationship between occupational status and voting is also interesting. Occupational status provides a good indicator of social class, and it shows that the middle class is significantly more likely to vote than the working class. The salariat or white-collar professionals, such as, doctors, lawyers and managers vote more than the routine non-manuals, for instance, clerical and administrative staff. The latter vote at about the same rate as the petty bourgeoise, or small businessmen and the self-employed, but both groups vote more than manual workers. The gap between the electoral participation of white-collar professionals and blue-collar manual workers in 2005 was almost 25 per cent.

The table shows considerably regional variations in turnout in 2005. Voters in the North and North West turned out in significantly fewer numbers than their counterparts in the South East and South West. A similar point can be made about voters in Scotland and Wales, although the differences between them and voters in the South East of England were less marked than differences between the North and South of England. The final sub-table in Table 3.1 shows that people who lived

Table 3.1   Turnout by social-demographic characteristics in 2005

	% Voted		% Voted
Age		**Occupational Status**	
18–25	43	Salariat	80
26–35	56	Routine non-manual	69
36–45	70	Petty bourgeoise	72
46–55	72	Foremen and technicians	61
56–65	83	Working class	57
66 plus	82		
Age completed education		**Region**	
15 or younger	71	East Anglia	64
16–18	67	East Midlands	62
19 or older	76	London	58
		North	58
Gender		North West	57
Men	66	South East	64
Women	70	South West	66
		West Midlands	60
Ethnicity		Yorkshire and Humberside	59
White British	69	Scotland	61
Other	56	Wales	62
Occupational Sector		**Housing Tenure**	
Private	64	Own outright	80
Public	78	Mortgage	71
Other	68	Rent	50

Source: British Election Study, 2005.

in rented accommodation were much less likely to vote than people who owned their own homes or had a mortgage.

The common denominator in the relationships set out in Table 3.1 is that people who are affluent, educated and who live in prosperous regions of the country tend to vote more than the people who lack these characteristics. In other words if the citizen has a large stake in the system in the form of a good job, a reasonable income, a home that is paid for in a prosperous neighbourhood, then they are more likely to vote than someone without these attributes. The idea that well-resourced individuals are more likely to participate than their less well-off counterparts is at the core of one of the leading theories of political participation, the civic voluntarism model (see Verba, Schlozman and Brady, 1995). This will be discussed further below.

Resources matter, but there is more to participation than material goods and social status, since voting, party activism, volunteering and consumer participation all involve choices of various kinds. It is apparent that some affluent, middle-class, home-owning citizens nonetheless choose not to vote, just as some poor, working-class, council tenants do vote. So we have to look beyond resources in order to get a full understanding of participation in contemporary Britain. We examine some theoretical explanations of why people vote in the next section.

Why do people vote?

There are a number of theories which have been used to explain political participation, and they can be divided into two broad classes. First, there are theories associated with sociological explanations of participation. These explain participation as being the product of social structures, social environments and the socialization experiences of individuals in early life. The common characteristic of such theories is that they emphasize the importance of social forces and structures, which are largely outside the control of the individual. In this view citizens are seen as being moulded by society and the social structures in which they are embedded. The second group of theories place individual choices at the centre of the stage, suggesting that participation is the consequence of the choices that individuals make arising from their preferences and values and in the context in which they find themselves. These play down the importance of social forces and social structures and emphasize the role of the citizen as an independent and autonomous individual who can choose from different alternatives on offer.

The civic voluntarism model is an example of the former type of sociological theory of participation. Sidney Verba and Norman Nie introduced this model in their study of participation in America more than forty years ago. They summarized it in the following quote:

> According to this model, the social status of an individual – his job, education, and income – determines to a large extent how much he participates. (Verba and Nie, 1972: 13)

Subsequent work has defined these resources as 'time, money and civic skills' (Verba, Schlozman and Brady, 1995: 271), and has incorporated additional motivational variables into the model. These motivational factors include the individual's psychological engagement with politics as well their sense of political efficacy or feelings that they can influence the system if they get involved (Verba, Schlozman and Brady,

1995: 272). However, these motivational variables are seen as being derived from the resources defined above, with the affluent and the educated being more motivated than the poor and uneducated. Thus motivations play a linking role between the individual's social characteristics on the one hand and their political involvement on the other.

Though developed in the context of American politics, the model was subsequently applied to the task of explaining cross-national political participation (Verba, Nie and Kim, 1978). This later work stressed the distinction between individual and group resources in explaining participation, arguing that: 'organization – and we might add ideology – is the weapon of the weak' (Verba, Nie and Kim 1978: 15). Thus ideological ties between individuals and institutions, such as, political parties and trade unions can compensate for a lack of individual resources, and boost participation. This means that the context in which individuals find themselves, and the organizations in which they belong, play an important role in explaining their involvement. Parry, Moyser and Day (1992) based their analysis of participation in Britain on this theoretical approach.

The civic voluntarism model is not the only sociological theory of participation, however. Another important theory of this type is social capital theory. The core idea here is that individuals who are embedded in strong networks of social relationships and who trust others are more likely to participate than their fellow citizens. We met social capital in Chapter 1 and the term was introduced into modern social theory by the sociologist James Coleman (1988, 1990). He argued that social interactions between people in voluntary settings help to generate 'credit slips' of mutual obligations, facilitate communication and foster norms of reciprocation. These in turn create trusting relationships between people.

Robert Putnam's work on social capital, mentioned in Chapter 2, shows that it can have many effects, but one of them is to stimulate political participation and voting (Putnam, 2000). If an individual trusts other people and works with them in a voluntary capacity, has many social ties and lives in a community with a great deal of voluntary activity going on, then that individual is more likely to vote. For most researchers, interpersonal trust is the key indicator of social capital (Fukuyama, 1995; Putnam, 1993, 2000; Brehm and Rahn, 1997). Such trust allows them to move beyond their own immediate circle of family members and friends and engage in cooperative behaviour with strangers. It follows that interactions between individuals in a voluntary setting help to generate interpersonal trust and this in turn creates social capital (Whiteley, 1999).

The second type of explanation of political participation is based on the idea that individuals will make choices to participate, given the right incentives and the right circumstances. Just as there are different sociological models of participation, there are different choice models as well. One such is the cognitive engagement model. The concept is that political participation is motivated by the individual's ability and willingness to process and understand information about politics and society (Norris, 2000; Clarke *et al.*, 2004; Dalton, 2005). In this model, factors such as the citizen's educational attainment, their knowledge of politics and attention to political events such as elections, as well as their overall engagement with the political process are the factors which explain their participation. Education is at the core of the model, since it increases the individual's ability to process and understand political information. The earlier discussion suggested that education is an important variable in the civic voluntarism model as well, but in that model it is a measure of resources. In the cognitive engagement model it plays a rather different role, as an indicator of the citizen's ability to make sense of the political world.

The modern political world is dominated by the media, particularly the electronic media. Since the costs of acquiring political information have fallen sharply over time because of the proliferation of media outlets it is easier than ever for the citizen to become well informed (Norris, 2000; Dalton, 2005). The growing number of television and radio channels and the twenty-four-hour news media and above all the rapid rise of the internet, make it relatively easy for individuals to become 'critical citizens' (Norris, 1999). Such individuals are not only relatively knowledgeable about politics, but they can evaluate the effectiveness of policies and judge the records of incumbent parties in delivering on their election promises. We return to this discussion in Chapter 6. Viewed from the perspective of political theory, cognitively engaged citizens are close to the classical Greek conception of the good citizen, who is an informed member of the *polis* and who fully participates in the process of government. The implication of this model is fairly straightforward in that the well-educated, knowledgeable and interested citizen will vote, and his uneducated, ignorant and uninterested counterpart will not.

A second model of participation in the choice tradition is the general incentives model, which is rooted in both rational choice and social-psychological accounts of human behaviour (Seyd and Whiteley, 1992, 2002; Whiteley and Seyd, 2002). This model was originally introduced to explain high-intensity forms of participation of the type undertaken by party activists. They are involved in running party organizations, setting up election campaigns, canvassing voters, attending political meetings, becoming candidates, and holding elected offices, all of which involve a considerable cost in time and energy. Therefore, at the core of the model is a cost-benefit calculation, the idea that individuals will participate if they feel that the benefits of doing so outweigh the costs.

In fact, if benefits and costs are narrowly defined, this gives rise to an awkward paradox in the literature on voting. The paradox is that if people make narrow calculations of the costs and benefits then nobody who is rational will vote. The logic behind this paradox is easy to describe. If a consumer wants a new car, for example, she will buy it if it has the features and performance she wants, and it is within her budget. So her choices and actions change the outcomes. The same logic cannot be applied to voting, however, because no individual can influence the outcome of an election in a UK constituency which typically consists of about 70,000 people. No elector can make the difference to whether or not one candidate rather than another wins in that particular constituency because there are so many other people involved. For this reason it is not rational to vote.

This point is reinforced by the fact that most constituencies in Britain are safe seats where the individual has even less of an incentive to vote, since there is an even smaller probability that their vote will change the outcome of the election. If citizens have no prospect of influencing the outcome then it is not rational for them to participate (Olson, 1965). The general incentive model circumvents this problem by incorporating a much wider set of incentives to participate than immediate costs and benefits, recognizing that, in practice, electors are not narrowly focused only on their own costs and benefits when they vote. These broader incentives include altruistic motives to participate, feelings that they have a moral duty to get involved and social norms, or the perception that what other people are doing influences their choices to participate.

An analysis of six rival models of participation applied to the task of explaining turnout in the 2001 British general election showed that no single model uniquely explained electoral participation (Clarke *et al*,. 2004: 237–77). Rather, both sociological and choice models each had something to contribute to the explanation of why people vote. However, the cognitive engagement and general incentives models together dominated the picture when it came to statistically explaining individual voting behaviour. Thus, factors such as the citizen's perceptions of the costs and benefits of voting, their levels of interest in the campaign, their knowledge of politics, and their feelings that they had a duty to vote largely explained their participation. Their social class, gender and ethnicity play a relatively minor role.

A full multivariate analysis of these different models is beyond the scope of this book, but we can illustrate the importance of three of the key variables in the cognitive engagement and general incentives models. We examined interest in politics in Chapter 2 and it turns out, not surprisingly, that this plays an important role in explaining why people vote. The British Election Study data from 2005 shows that there was a 60 percentage point difference in turnout between those who reported being very interested and those who said they were not at all interested in politics. Just over 80 per cent of those who were very interested in politics voted compared with only just over 20 per cent of those not at all interested.

Another key variable is the citizen's perception that they have a duty to vote in elections. A sense of civic duty has a very strong influence on electoral turnout with just over 80 per cent of respondents who strongly agree that 'it is every citizen's duty to vote' turning out in the general election compared with just over 20 per cent who strongly disagree with the statement. We saw in Table 3.1 that there is a big gap between the participation of young people and older people in Britain and this gap has been growing wider over time (Clarke *et al.*, 2009). A key reason for this is that young people no longer have the sense of civic duty of their older counterparts. They don't recognize that voting is something that a 'good citizen' should do and so they increasingly do not turn out to vote.

A third very important variable which explains turnout is party identification, that is, the psychological attachment that some people have to a political party. Individuals who strongly identify with a political party are more than two-and-half times more likely to vote than individuals who do not identify with any party at all. Therefore, partisanship plays an important role in encouraging people to vote and this is an important factor in choice models of participation. It is clear that one of the key reasons why turnout is declining is because citizen attachments to political parties have been weakening for many years. We discuss this development more fully below.

These findings are consistent with the idea that citizens have an increasingly instrumental orientation towards politics, and choose the mode of participation which is most likely to achieve their objectives (Thomassen, 2004). Citizens will vote if there is a real choice between the parties and if they feel that it makes a difference to outcomes as to which party wins the election. The same type of instrumental motives will encourage some people to get involved in single-issue pressure groups such as Greenpeace or Oxfam, if the environment or third-world poverty is what they really care about. Others will participate in community action groups in their area, if they perceive their interests to be at stake. This often gives rise to so-called NIMBY (Not In My Back Yard) participation in which people oppose local planning decisions that might adversely affect the value of their properties. Essentially, such individuals are unlikely to participate merely because they have the resources to do so or because they are rich in social capital, although these factors will play a role in their decisions. Rather, they will get involved if they have a combination of the incentives and levels of engagement together which serve to trigger political action.

Given this overview of the factors which explain participation, how can we explain the decline in voting behaviour seen in Figure 3.2? This is discussed in the next section.

Why has voting declined?

The earlier discussion suggests that three broad factors are at work in explaining why voting has declined in Britain over time. The first is derived from sociological theories and argues that changes in society have detached citizens from the political process. The second derives from the cognitive engagement model and suggests that individuals have lost interest in the political process and in elections. The third relates to the general incentives model and argues that citizens face declining incentives to get involved in politics and to vote, and this has reduced their rates of participation. We can investigate these three alternatives by examining changes in key variables over time by looking at British Election Study surveys from 1974 and then comparing them with the survey from the 2005. This provides a period of more than thirty years over which changes can be explored. The aim will be to look for variables which have changed significantly over time. Clearly, if a measure is a significant predictor of voting but it has not changed much, then it cannot be an explanation of declining participation. We discuss each of the three factors in turn.

Changes in the social structure

The earlier discussion suggested that individuals who are educated and have high social status are more likely to participate than the uneducated and with low status. We can get some idea of the magnitude of the changes in these variables by comparing data from the 1974 and 2005 British Election Studies. We have concentrated on the two sociological characteristics which have really changed over the 30-year period. The first is education, with a massive growth in higher education occurring between these two dates. Only 4.5 per cent of the respondents in the 1974 study reported being graduates, compared with 23.6 per cent reporting this in 2005. Thus the number of graduates identified in the surveys increased by a factor of five over this 30-year period. At the other end of the scale the number of people who left school at the minimum age of sixteen fell from 72 per cent in 1974 to 29 per cent in 2005.

Alongside this, was another important development, a significant decline in working-class occupations and a rise in middle-class occupations in the workforce. In 1974 some 61 per cent of respondents in the election study survey had working-class occupations and 19 per cent reported having middle-class occupations. By 2005 this had changed completely, with 39 per cent reporting that they had working-class occupations, exactly the same percentage who reported being in middle-class occupations. In terms of occupational status, Britain became much more of a middle-class society by 2005 than it was thirty years earlier.

These findings do of course give rise to a paradox, since the civic voluntarism model predicts that turnout along with other forms of participation should have risen rather than fallen as a consequence of these trends. So there is clearly something wrong with this model as an explanation of citizen participation. This apparent paradox can be accounted for by a theoretical analysis which has emerged from the literature on civic education. The explanation is that political participation is driven by the individual's relative social status rather than by their absolute status (see Brody, 1978; Nie, Junn and Stehlik-Barry, 1996). To clarify this point, absolute status refers to a person's income, their occupational status and their educational attainments. This is what drives political participation according to the civic voluntarism model, so if a person is wealthier, has a higher status occupation and is more highly educated than the average citizen they will participate more.

However, if participation depends on their relative status this may no longer be true. Relative status refers to the individual's position in the social structure relative to everyone else. Viewed from this perspective, if everyone becomes more affluent, more highly educated and acquires a more highly paid occupation, this will not increase their social status relative to everyone else, because everyone is moving up the status ladder together. In this situation their position in the social structure will not have changed and if this actually what drives their participation, then they will not necessarily get more involved. The economist Fred Hirsch discussed this idea in the 1970s, when he wrote: 'To the extent that education conveys information about the innate or acculturated relative capacity of the individual who has undergone it, more education for all leaves everyone in the same place' (Hirsch, 1976: 49).

This relative interpretation of status implies that participation in Britain will not necessarily increase as incomes and middle-class occupations grow over time. In fact, one implication of the relative status idea is that citizen involvement will diminish among those who get left behind in the drive for increased status. While it is true that there are many more graduates and middle-class occupations in Britain in the twenty-first century in comparison with the 1970s, there is also a large number of people who are not graduates and who do not have middle-class occupations. In a world of relative status, a working-class person who left school at aged fifteen has a lower status in 2005 than they would have had in 1974, because there are many more people above them in the status hierarchy.

In addition, growing income inequality in society means a further loss of status for many people, which is also likely to reduce their participation if relative status is what really counts. Between the mid-1970s and the mid-2000s, income inequality in Britain increased by just over 20 per cent (see http://stats.oecd.org/). Thus, it is possible to explain part of the decline in participation by changes in the social structure and trends in inequality over the last thirty years. We return to this point in a later chapter.

There is another development which has implications for electoral participation, and that is changes in the relationship between social status and partisanship. The first comprehensive analysis of voting behaviour in Britain by Butler and Stokes set out in their book *Political Change in Britain* (1974) emphasized the importance of partisanship in electoral politics. Partisanship derives from the idea that: 'most electors think of themselves as supporters of a given party in a lasting sense' (Butler and Stokes, 1974: 39) and their partisanship makes it possible for the voters to make sense of electoral politics. It is seen as a long-term psychological attachment to one or other of the political parties, and it is the most enduring feature of voters' political beliefs. In this model, partisanship is the product of enduring social cleavages, principally social class, and it is transmitted across the generations by means of socialization processes within the family – it drives electoral politics.

In a much quoted passage written in 1967 Peter Pulzer argued that 'class is the basis of British Party politics: all else is embellishment and detail' (1967: 98). In other words, in the 1960s most middle-class people identified with and voted for the Conservative party and most working-class people did the same for Labour, although there were always exceptions.

One of the implications of the Butler–Stokes analysis is that if the relationship between social class and partisanship weakens, it going to affect voting behaviour. If partisanship ceases to be anchored in social cleavages and weakens, this will discourage electoral participation. Thus trends in the relationship between social class and partisanship may be important factors for understanding declining turnouts over time. We will postpone a discussion of trends in partisanship to the next section and concentrate on the relationship between class and partisanship here. The important relationships are set out in Table 3.2, which shows how occupational status and partisanship were linked in 1974 and again in 2005.

Table 3.2 shows that in 1974 about half of the people in middle-class occupations identified with the Conservatives, just under a fifth of them identified with Labour, and about one in six of them identified with the Liberals. A very small number of people identified with minor parties and just over 12 per cent identified with no party at all. The distribution of partisanship for the working class was rather different, with just under a third identifying with the Conservatives and around 45 per identifying with Labour. In addition just over 12 per cent identified with the Liberals. Again, identification with minor parties was very small and just under 10 per cent of the working class identified with no party at all.

If we move forward thirty years, the picture changes dramatically. In 2005 less than a third of the middle classes identified with the Conservatives and a larger proportion of them, just over a third, identified with Labour. Liberal Democrat identification among middle-class electors was down slightly compared with 1974, but middle-class identification with other parties, or no party at all, increased over time. Looking at working-class electors in 2005, those who identified with the Conservatives fell below one in five, while the proportion that identified with Labour remained about the same as thirty years earlier. Again, Liberal Democrat identification among the working class fell slightly and almost one in five working-class electors identified with no party. Clearly, the relationship between partisanship and social class weakened considerably over this thirty-year period. The middle classes were no longer predominantly Conservative in 2005, and the growth in non-identification among the working class means that their support for political

Table 3.2   Social class and partisanship in 1974 and 2005

1974	Conservatives	Labour	Liberals	Other parties	None or DK	
Middle class	49.3	19.4	16.8	1.6	12.8	100%
Intermediate class	49.7	22.1	15.5	1.0	11.8	100%
Working class	31.1	44.5	12.6	2.0	9.8	100%

2005	Conservatives	Labour	Liberal Democrats	Other parties	None or DK	
Middle class	30.6	33.5	13.6	45.7	16.7	100%
Intermediate class	30.8	32.6	15.3	3.9	17.4	100%
Working class	19.6	44.0	10.3	6.6	19.4	100%

Source: British Election Study, February 1974 and 2005.

parties weakened too, even though many of them continued to identify with Labour.

It is important to remember the earlier point that the class composition of the workforce has changed dramatically over time, with many more middle-class occupations and fewer working-class occupations in the workforce. The meaning of social class, in so far as it is measured by occupational status, has changed and if the relative status thesis is correct it has weakened considerably as a predictor of voting behaviour. One of the implications of this trend is that this will tend to discourage turnout because voting is no longer anchored in the social circumstances in which people find themselves. In a world of strong class identities, party loyalty is likely to be part of those identities and strong attachments will make people vote. In a world of 'pick and mix' politics which are not anchored in social structures people are likely to see voting as an optional choice rather than an expression of their identities.

Changes in the social structure over time are clearly important for explaining changes in participation, but they only go some way towards explaining the decline in voting. It is obvious that relatively gradual changes in society cannot explain the sudden drop in turnout between 1997 and 2001 observed in Figure 3.2. Clearly, other more short-term factors are at work in explaining this, and we turn to these next.

Changes in citizen engagement

The cognitive engagement model explains participation in terms of the individual's willingness and ability to acquire and process political information. The growth in higher education discussed earlier means that the ability of the average citizen to deal with political information should have increased, but this says nothing about their willingness to acquire such information. A comparison of the 1974 and 2005 election studies shows that interest in politics rose over this period from 62 per cent to 72 per cent, and the percentage of people who cared which party won the election similarly increased from 68 per cent to 74 per cent. So it appears that engagement with the political process has risen over time.

However, the same point cannot be made about the strength of partisanship which has declined sharply over this period. In 1974 some 90 per cent of the respondents in the election study survey were very or fairly strong partisans, but by 2005 the figure was 56 per cent. In the earlier discussion we pointed out that there is a huge difference in the voting turnout of strongly attached partisans compared with the unattached. Given this, a weakening of partisanship will reduce turnout over time. Therefore,the failure of the mainstream parties to retain the loyalty of voters is one of the key reasons why we observe a decline in electoral participation. Clearly, this has implications for other forms of participation such as party membership, protest rallies and campaigning, insofar as grassroots party organizations play a role in supporting such activities.

To understand a bit more about what motivated this decline of partisanship we can draw on some indicators in the 1974 and 2005 election studies, which asked voters if they perceived differences between the parties and then queried further on the nature of these differences. In 1974, 33 per cent of respondents stated that they perceived a 'great deal of difference' between the political parties, but by 2005 this had narrowed to 22 per cent. Given that the New Labour project was designed to leave old Labour behind and to capture the middle ground of British politics this is not surprising. However, from the point of view of electoral turnout, a narrowing of the differences between the parties is likely to discourage some people from voting since they increasingly perceive that there is no real choice on offer.

Table 3.3 identifies perceptions of the characteristics of parties among the public in 1974 and again in 2005, and it is revealing in helping to explain the malaise in which the parties find themselves. It appears that there has been a massive growth in scepticism about the trustworthiness

Table 3.3   Perceptions of the two major parties in 1974 and 2005

	Conservatives		Labour	
	1974	*2005*	*1974*	*2005*
Keeps promises	50.7	29.0	49.8	23.9
Breaks promises	36.7	71.0	36.0	76.1
Capable	64.5	47.0	62.2	66.1
Not capable	24.3	53.0	25.0	33.9
Usually trust	28.1	7.6	21.6	14.1
Rarely trust	19.3	39.6	16.8	36.8

Note: Trust in the parties in the 2005 survey was recoded from a 0 to 10 scale with respondents giving the parties a score of 8 to 10 described as 'usually' trusting, and respondents giving them a score of 0 to 3 as 'rarely' trusting.

Source: British Election Study, February 1974 and 2005.

and honesty of the two major parties. In 1974, approximately half the electorate felt that the Conservatives and Labour kept their promises. By 2005 this was down to under a third in the case of the Conservatives and under a quarter in the case of Labour. The evidence on trustworthiness tells a similar story. In 1974 close to 30 per cent of the electorate felt that they could trust the Conservatives and just over a fifth felt that they could trust Labour. This had declined rather dramatically by 2005.

Interestingly enough, the data on perceptions of competence or capability tells a different story, since more electors thought that Labour was capable in 2005 than thought this in 1974. By the same token, while perceptions of the capability of the Conservatives did fall over the period, close to half of the respondents thought that the party was capable in 2005. Clearly, many people still think that the parties are capable, but they just don't trust them and this is one of the underlying reasons why many people do not vote.

Changes in the incentives to participate

There are a number of different incentives which are important for stimulating turnout and political participation. One such incentive relates to the political differences between the parties. If such differences are very large, then both supporters and opponents of the parties have a strong incentive to turn out and vote. This is because there is more at stake in the election in policy terms than when the gap between parties is narrow. When the two major parties are close together in policy terms, then it doesn't really matter which one gets elected from the point of view of the average voter. A similar point can be made about party leaders. There is more at stake when the leaders appear to be very different than when they appear to be rather similar to each other.

We noted earlier that a third of respondents in the 1974 election survey thought that there were large differences between the parties, and by 2005 this was down to a just over a fifth. However, about half of the respondents in the later study thought that there were some differences between parties, so perceptions of policy differences between the political parties have not disappeared altogether, but they have weakened considerably over time. Again this will reduce the incentive to vote if people have the impression that parties differ only marginally between each other. If electors think that the policies delivered will be rather similar, regardless of who is elected, then they are unlikely to go to the polls. A second development which is similar to the first is a narrowing of perceived differences between the party leaders. In the election study, survey respondents were asked to evaluate the party leaders on a scale from zero to ten. The difference in these marks between the Labour and Conservative leaders in 1974 was 0.8, but it had declined to 0.5 by 2005, a fall of nearly half.

Actually, it would be surprising if perceived differences between the parties and leaders had not declined over time, since both Labour and the Conservatives were trying hard to capture the middle ground of politics by 2005. The creation of New Labour was a conscious attempt to reinvent the party with the aim of broadening its electoral appeal by shifting to the centre. Similarly, the loss of two general elections in 1997 and again in 2001 encouraged the Conservatives to shift to more centrist positions in the political spectrum.

This last point is supported by independent evidence derived from an entirely different source than surveys. This appears in Figure 3.4, which used data from the Comparative Manifesto Project to plot the ideological position of political parties over time (Klingemann, Budge and Barro, 2006). The Manifesto Project involves coding the policy commitments made by political parties in their election manifestos into a single left–right political dimension, and so it shows how left-wing or right-wing the parties are in terms of their policy commitments at each election since the war. The distance between the parties on the left–right scale in February 1974 was 48.5, and this declined to 17.5, or just over a third of the earlier score, by the 2005 election. The chart shows how Labour shifted to the right and the Conservatives to the left after the 1983 election and reached their closest point in 2001, which coincided with the lowest turnout in the post-war period of 59.4 per cent. It is note-

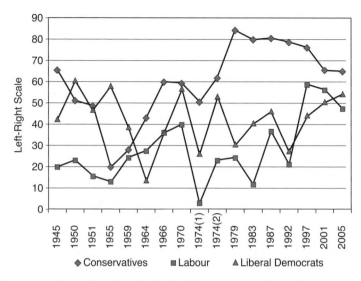

Note: A high score on the left–right scale means that the party was to the right of the political spectrum in that election.

Source: Klingemann, Budge and Barro, 2006.

Figure 3.4 Left–right scale scores for the political parties, 1945–2005

worthy that the turnout in the February 1974 was 78.1 per cent and in 2005 was 61.2 per cent, indicating that there is a relationship between policy differences and turnout. The clear implication is that when there is less at stake fewer people vote.

Another phenomenon, which is likely to undermine the incentive to vote is the perception that the election is a forgone conclusion because one party is clearly going to win. The published opinion polls during an election campaign have a fairly good track record in predicting the outcome of elections with relatively small errors (Butler and Butler, 2006:132–3). There are many polls conducted during the campaigns and commentators draw the public's attention to the competitiveness of the contest, so most of the electorate will have a good idea which party is going to win if the parties are not too close together. If the outcome of the election is something of a forgone conclusion then it is likely to deter voting since many people will regard the election, in effect, as having already taken place. They will conclude that their fellow-citizens have already decided which party is going to win. This phenomenon is the national counterpart to the well-known pattern of turnouts being higher in marginal seats where elections are competitive than in safe seats where they are not (Denver, 2003). It was clearly very influential during the 2001 general election when the pre-election polls all predicted a large Labour victory, and this in turn explains why turnout was at a post-war low in that election. Turnout increased, though not by much, in 2010 when the outcome of the election was uncertain and most polls were predicting a hung Parliament.

Conclusion

This chapter has examined political participation in Britain over time, paying particular attention to electoral participation, which is at the heart of democratic politics. We have seen that turnouts have been declining in Britain and identified some of the factors which explain this trend. Changes in the social structure, which have disconnected political parties from their class bases are partly responsible, as is the decline in political parties as objects of identification by voters. Other factors linked to the incentives to participate are also influential, particularly the decline in ideological differences between the parties and the predictability of elections in which one party dominates the other, a feature of the three elections between 1997 and 2005.

Political parties play a key role in explaining these developments. They are less and less recognized as objects of loyalty by the average voter, and this is in part prompted by the fact that fewer people see major differences between them or between their leaders. In many ways, political parties are the glue that holds the British system of government together and so in the next chapter we explore in more detail what has been happening to these parties to try to understand why these developments have occurred.

4

Political Parties and Grassroots Activism

The previous chapter showed that changes in political parties are one of the key factors in explaining the decline in electoral participation that has been occurring in Britain over time. They are also contributing to the decline of other forms of participation, a topic discussed more fully below. Given this conclusion, the aim of this chapter is to look closely at changes which have occurred in British political parties, to get a sense of how important these are for the civic culture. It is essential to remember that political parties are not single entities but are complex organizations, which operate at different levels of the political system. They exist in the minds of voters as objects of identification or indifference and, at this level, they influence electoral behaviour.

Parties are also voluntary organizations, which operate in the community through the work of activists and members who make a contribution to electoral participation by campaigning and in local government. More generally at this level, parties help to link local and national governments with ordinary citizens. In this sense local party volunteers are 'ambassadors in the community' (Scarrow, 1996). There is also a third level at which parties are important, and that is in central government. They are the 'glue' that holds the executive together and ensures that decision making is possible under the Westminster constitutional model. At this level the focus is on party organization and party discipline in Parliament.

The importance of parties

Parties are important to the political system because they fulfil a variety of crucial functions. If they didn't exist, they would have to be invented, such is their importance to the political system. The role of parties in the British political system was discussed in some detail in the Houghton Report, a government inquiry conducted more than a generation ago (HMSO, 1976). The Houghton committee was tasked with the function of examining financial support for political parties, and it was anxious to spell out why parties are important. It argued that:

> [Parties] provide the framework within which different political views can be formulated, debated and translated into practical political programmes, and the many demands and efforts of smaller groups in society can be aggregated and merged into a small number of workable alternative political programmes. (HMSO, 1976: 18)

The aggregation of interests is probably the most important function that parties fulfil. If there were no institutions tasked with aggregating the many diverse interests in British society and formulating their demands into workable policy proposals and subsequently into legislation, then government could not function. Parties are unique in this respect and certainly very different from interest groups. The latter usually have a much narrower focus concerned with winning benefits for their members or the groups they represent and, moreover, they do not aspire to govern the country. In the British political system, government would not work without political parties, a fact that has been recognized for a long time. In a speech to the House of Commons delivered in August 1848, Benjamin Disraeli argued:

> You cannot choose between party government and Parliamentary government. I say you can have no Parliamentary government if you have no party government; and therefore when gentlemen denounce party government, they strike at the scheme of government which in my opinion has made this country great. (Platte, 1991)

Without political parties, each piece of legislation before Parliament would require the construction of a new majority coalition. This coalition would have to be painstakingly assembled by the sponsors of a Parliamentary Bill and this would inevitably mean compromises and amendments that are likely to make the subsequent legislation more complex and less coherent. This activity of building coalitions would have to be done for each and every Bill, making legislation for controversial issues difficult, if not impossible, to achieve. In a Parliament without parties, MPs would be very willing to support spending which brings benefits to their constituents, but they would be much more reluctant to support the taxation which pays for such spending. From their point of view it would always be better to get the benefits of collective action for their constituents while at the same time passing on the costs of such actions to other people. This exercise of trying to concentrate the benefits on to support groups while at the same time seeking to spread the costs across society as a whole makes legislators irresponsible in the absence of parties. One of the most important functions of parties, therefore, is to reconcile decision makers into accepting the costs of political actions and government decision making, as well as the benefits.

Parties also have other important functions. They allow politicians to learn their trade by socializing them into the bargaining, debating and deal-making which are essential parts of politics and the decision-making process. It is within party organizations that apprentice politicians learn the skills they will need to be effective. Another important function supported by parties is the recruitment of politicians. The local party organizations in Britain play a key role in selecting candidates for office in Parliamentary and Local Government elections. A local connection by a candidate can be a prized asset when it comes to seeking elected office, so party 'selectorates' play an important role in recruiting local notables into the political process.

Parties also simplify the choices for voters, by providing 'heuristics' or rules of thumb which citizens can use to make sense of the political choices they face at election time. These have been described as 'fast and frugal' heuristics (Gigerenzer and Todd, 1999). In the absence of party labels on the ballot paper, the average voter would be very hard put to distinguish between the different candidates in an election. Since the great majority of voters do not know their candidates personally and therefore have little information on whom they should support, electoral choice would become very difficult. The likelihood is that candidates with a large budget for publicity, or who were already celebrities, would win. Party labels change this situation by associating candidates with broad party programmes that are understood by most people and therefore greatly facilitate the task facing voters in deciding whom to support in elections.

Again, in relation to elections, political parties are campaigning organizations, both at the national and local levels in elections for local councils, the Parliaments at Westminster and in Scotland and Wales, and also for the European Parliament. The role of party leaders in campaigning has always been recognized in the voting literature, but relatively recent research has established the importance of local campaigning by party activists and supporters in helping to increase turnout and persuade floating voters to support their party (Seyd and Whiteley, 1992; Johnston and Pattie, 1995; Denver and Hands, 1997; Clarke *et al.*, 2004, 2009).

Party organizations have the important function of mobilizing voters and in marginal constituencies they can make the difference between winning and losing.

Another important function of political parties is to 'organise disappointment', that is to reconcile citizens, who are on the losing side in policy debates and in elections, to accept defeat (Whiteley and Seyd, 2002). Parties encourage citizens to believe that while they may be on the losing side on one occasion, they can be on the winning side on another, which can help to reconcile losers in the political process to their situation and thereby keep politics non-violent. If parties did not exist then it is difficult to see how this function would be fulfilled and consequently, politics would be a lot more conflicted.

Finally, parties play an important role in communicating policy alternatives to the electorate, thereby greatly facilitating policy making. Much of government is about persuading people to change their behaviour in various ways. Examples include encouraging people to stop smoking and to lose weight for health reasons; persuading people to reduce their carbon footprints and adopt environmentally friendly lifestyles in order to combat climate change; reducing anti-social behaviour by encouraging social norms which sanction such behaviour, and so on. Much of successful policy making involves communication and persuasion, for which parties are key organizations.

With these distinctions in mind we examine trends in the role and importance of political parties at the different levels of the political system, starting with parties and the voters.

Parties and voters

Chapter 3 revealed how important parties are for sustaining political participation. One the most well-documented finding in electoral research in Britain is the long running decline in voter attachments to political parties (Sarlvik and Crewe, 1983; Franklin, 1985). The extent to which individual citizens identify with political parties has been inexorably weakening for almost half a century. This is evident in Figure 4.1, which uses data from British Election Study Surveys conducted since 1964 to measure the strength of voter attachments to political parties. The vertical axis in the figure is a measure of the strength of partisanship which varies from 0 to 3 and is derived from identical questions asked in each election study. There is a remarkably consistent decline in voter attachments to political parties over this period. Parti-

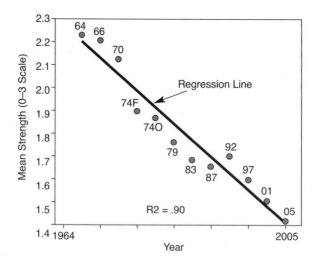

Note: 0 = non-supporter; 1 = not very strong party supporter; 2 = fairly strong party supporter;
3 = very strong party supporter.

Source: BES Surveys 1964 to 2005.

Figure 4.1   Changes in the strength of partisanship in Britain, 1964–2005

sanship has weakened by about 40 per cent over this period of forty
years – in effect, 1 per cent a year.

One of the effects of this trend is to make electoral behaviour more
volatile and more dependent on election campaigns. One indicator of
this is the timing of the vote decision by individual electors. In 1964,
one of the earliest election study surveys showed that some 12 per cent
of respondents made up their minds about which party to support during
the month-long official election campaign, but about 77 per cent had
done so in the years before the election took place. Clearly, the scope
for influencing the outcome by campaigning was very limited at that
time. However by 2005 this had all changed. In that year, 34 per cent
reported making up their minds during the campaign and only 52 per
cent reported doing this in the years prior to the election. Thus, the final
stages of the campaign have become more and more important to electoral politics.

Electoral volatility aside, perhaps the most important consequence of
declining partisanship is that it weakens the incentives to turnout and
vote. If an individual is a strong partisan and they acquired their party

loyalty in early life, they will have a strong incentive to vote. This was apparent from the evidence in Chapter 3, which showed that declining partisanship played a major role in explaining a decline in general election turnouts.

A third effect of weakening partisanship, which has implications for governance in Britain, is the growth in support for parties other than Labour and the Conservatives, the two parties which have alternated in government for the last century or more. It is clear from Figure 4.2 that successive governments have been elected to power with ever smaller percentages of the electorate. Figure 4.2 shows that when Labour was elected in the landslide election of 1945 it captured 35 per cent of the electorate. When the Conservatives won the election of 1951 they did so with 40 per cent. Mrs Thatcher's election victory of 1979, which had major consequences for British politics, was achieved with 33 per cent of the electorate. Tony Blair's victory of 1997 which was equally consequential for British politics was achieved with 31 per cent, and his third term victory in 2005 was obtained with only 22 per cent. This trend decline in the size of the electoral mandates of successive governing parties in Britain is the product of lower turnouts, but also arises from the increase in support for the other parties, notably the Liberal Democrats and the Nationalists in Wales and Scotland. In that respect, the 2010 general election was a watershed since electoral support for the two major parties reached such a low level at 65 per cent of the vote that neither of them was elected with an outright majority, and so a coalition government emerged.

Relatively little attention has been paid to this trend in discussions of British politics, and successive governments have continued to rule as though they had a mandate from a majority of the electorate. In fact, this development implies that governments have become less and less legitimate over time, given that they are supported by dwindling proportions of citizens. The theme of the relationship between the effectiveness of government and political support is taken up in Chapter 7, but it suggests that these trends have undermined the effectiveness of British government.

Overall, the weakening of political parties in the minds of the voters increasingly undermines the 'mandate' theory of government, discussed in Chapter 1. People are less sure about the party they are voting for and fewer of them are voting, therefore, it becomes harder and harder to argue that a newly elected government has a 'mandate' to implement its programme, particularly if that programme is very controversial.

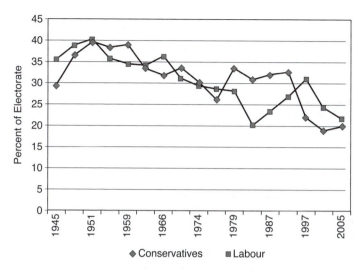

Source: Electoral Commission, see http://www.electoralcommission.org.uk/.

Figure 4.2   Conservative and Labour vote shares of the electorate, 1945–2005

Parties and activists

Turning next to political parties as voluntary organizations, there is good evidence to show that a long-term decline in voluntary activity in political parties has been taking place in Britain over the years that partisanship in the electorate has weakened (Seyd and Whiteley, 1992, 2002; Whiteley, Seyd and Richardson, 1994; Whiteley and Seyd, 2002; Whiteley, Seyd and Billinghurst, 2006). Webb (2000: 193) showed that, in 1964, individual membership of the Labour party was just above 830,000 but this had halved to just over 400,000 by 1997. Comparable figures for the Conservatives were 2,150,000 members in 1964 and 400,000 in 1997. A similar pattern applies to the Liberals/Liberal Democrats with a membership of nearly 280,000 in 1964 declining to 100,000 by 1997.

In this section we examine this issue more closely by looking at the state of the grassroots party organizations in Britain with the assistance of a large-scale internet survey conducted in January 2008 (Whiteley, 2009). The aim of the survey was to track changes in membership over time and to compare and contrast the health of the grassroots party mem-

Table 4.1   Party membership in Britain, 2008, (N=1,230)

Party	Percentage of members	Percentage vote in the 2005 General Election
Labour	38.4	36.1
Conservatives	30.6	33.2
Liberal Democrats	13.7	22.6
Scottish National Party	3.6	1.6
Plaid Cymru	0.6	0.7
Green Party	2.5	1.1
UK Independence Party	4.7	2.3
Respect	0.4	0.3
British National Party	2.2	0.7
Other parties	3.3	1.3

Sources: BES Continuous Monitoring Survey, 2008; Electoral Commission; see http://www.electoral-commission.org.uk

bership organizations. The survey confirms that trends first identified in the 1990s are continuing up to the present time.

The 2008 survey was conducted on the internet and was able to iden-tify party members in the electorate by interviewing a very large number of citizens (see Whiteley, 2009). Table 4.1 shows the percentage of members of each party identified in the survey, and it is compared with the vote shares obtained by these parties in the General Election of 2005. The survey contained 1,230 party members and at that time Labour had the largest share of them. It appears that the party had a slightly bigger share of the party members in Britain than it had voters in the general election. However, for Conservatives it was the other way round. On the other hand, the discrepancies between vote shares and party mem-bership shares were not large for either party.

The same point may not be made about the Liberal Democrats, however, since in their case the discrepancy between members and voters was quite large. The Liberal Democrat vote share was almost twice as large as their party membership share. In the case of other parties, the Scottish National Party did well in terms of having a greater proportion of members than voters, as did UKIP, the Green Party and the British National Party. Clearly, there is an association between elec-toral success and the ability of a party to recruit members, although this association is far from being perfect.

One important political consideration is the strength of party attach-ments of the party members. We should normally expect party members to have much stronger attachments to their party than the voters in general, but variations in the strength of attachment can be taken as an

Table 4.2 The strength of partisanship of party members in Britain, 2008

Strength of partisanship	Labour	Conservative	Liberal Democrat
Very strong	61.2	55.7	57.4
Fairly strong	34.3	39.5	33.1
Not very strong	4.1	4.5	9.5
Don't know	0.4	0.3	0

Source: Internet survey (BES, 2008).

indicator of their willingness to support their party by voting for it, donating money to it, and campaigning for it in an election. Table 4.2 shows the strength of partisanship of Labour, Conservative and Liberal Democrat party members. It is clear that Labour party members had stronger attachments than Conservatives or Liberal Democrats at the time of the survey. More than 61 per cent of Labour members had very strong attachments compared with only 56 per cent of Conservatives and 57 per cent of Liberal Democrats. At the other end of the scale the Liberal Democrats had more than twice as many members who were not strongly attached than their main rivals. Of the three parties, therefore, the Liberal Democrats were the most weakly attached, which has implications for the amount of money they can raise from members and the number of volunteers they can mobilize during election campaigns.

What does this survey tell us about changes in party membership over time? It contained almost twice as many former party members as current members. The percentages of ex-party members appear in Table 4.3 which is the counterpart to Table 4.1. The striking finding from this table is than more than 40 per cent of the ex-members were formerly in the Labour party. While Labour may have had more current members than any of the other parties, it has also had far more former members. This is an interesting finding, and to put it in perspective, there were 472 current Labour party members in the sample, and no less than 1,093 former Labour party members a ratio of 2.3 ex-members to every member. The equivalent ratio of ex-members to members for the Conservatives was 1.9 and for the Liberal Democrats it was 2.0. It is striking that ex-members outnumbered current members for every party in Table 4.3 with one exception – the British National Party – which appeared to be the only party growing in size in 2008.

Insight into when the ex-members left their respective parties can be obtained from Table 4.4. This shows the average percentage of members who left the party in successive periods over time. Thus the number of Labour party members who left their party peaked in the second term

Table 4.3   Former party members in Britain, 2008 (N=2,288)

Party	Percentage of ex-members
Labour	42.9
Conservatives	27.8
Liberal Democrats	13.2
Scottish National Party	2.9
Plaid Cymru	0.9
Green Party	1.8
UK Independence Party	2.6
Respect	0.2
British National Party	0.4
Other parties	7.2

Source: Internet survey (BES, 2008).

of the Labour government between 2001 and 2005. This coincided with the start of the Iraq war and the upsurge in protest demonstrations which occurred throughout Britain, together with the growing unpopularity of the Prime Minister, Tony Blair. However a sizeable number left the party in Labour's first term between 1997 and 2001. Part of the reason for this is that Tony Blair led a campaign to recruit new members after he became party leader in 1994. This was quite successful and it increased the size of the party membership by some 40 per cent (Seyd and Whiteley, 2002). However, many of these new recruits were not strongly attached to the party and left once the party leadership, paying much less attention to the grassroots party, became pre-occupied with governing after 1997.

More generally, party members left in greater numbers after Labour came into power than when the party was in opposition. However, it would be wrong to conclude that parties always have difficulty retaining members only when they are in government. This is because the Conservatives' loss of membership peaked in 2006 when 10.6 per cent of the sample left the party. This coincided with the first full year of David Cameron's leadership, suggesting that many people in the grassroots party were dissatisfied with his modernization strategy at that time. It is also apparent that the Liberal Democrats lost a number of members in that year and, again, this roughly coincided with the period when Menzies Campbell was the party leader. He became party leader in March 2006 but stepped down in December 2007, and was generally considered ineffective, subsequently being replaced by Nick Clegg.

What then are the implications of these findings for British politics in general and for political parties in particular? The interesting question

Table 4.4 Percentage of members leaving each year in each party

When leaving former party	Labour	Conservatives	Liberal Democrats
2007	1.6	1.3	1.2
2006	4.9	10.6	9.0
Between 2001 and 2005	6.4	5.7	6.0
Between 1997 and 2001	5.3	2.8	3.7
Between 1992 and 1997	2.6	2.9	2.4
Between 1979 and 1992	1.5	1.5	1.8

Source: Internet survey (BES, 2008).

is the extent to which the functions of parties explored in the Houghton Report, referred to earlier, are supported by the voluntary activities of party members. Clearly, political parties can continue to aggregate interests and provide coherence to Parliamentary organizations in the absence of local party members. Broadly speaking, parties at the centre can continue to function without the volunteers. But it is hard to see how parties can function effectively in the wider community without their voluntary organizations. As the earlier discussion indicates, grassroots party members select and socialize the candidates for elective office, they stimulate citizen participation in politics by campaigning, they help to provide political education by acting as 'ambassadors in the community', and they help to fund local activities and elections. In a world in which party finance is increasing tightly regulated and where there is public resistance to further state aid to political parties, it is apparent that parties really depend on their volunteers to raise money. Clearly, there are many important functions fulfilled by party members, which will not be effectively performed if their numbers continue to decline.

A further aspect of the role of party members, which has not been recognized much in the literature, is their function in supporting political participation and political communication in Britain. This is discussed in the next section.

Party supporters and political participation

In Chapter 3 we examined a number of different forms of political participation in Britain and in Figure 3.1 showed that apart from voting, political participation was a minority activity. While activities, such as signing petitions and boycotting goods for political reasons may be minority activities, they are large minorities involving millions of people. Moreover, the numbers involved in consumer forms of participation are growing all the time. Even in relation to activities, such as demonstrating and contacting politicians, where relatively small proportions of the population get involved, these are nonetheless very important to the political system. If no-one contacted politicians or public officials, for example, then it is hard to see how they could fulfil the function of representing citizens in the policy-making process. Equally, if nobody helped in charitable organizations as volunteers then large areas of the welfare state would become unviable, since they are supported by volunteers. Most importantly, if no-one worked for, or supported, political parties at election time, the political system would become ungovernable for reasons discussed earlier.

These considerations lead to an important question. How important are political parties in the task of supporting and underpinning political participation in Britain? What would participation look like if nobody supported a party? This issue can be investigated by examining the contribution of party supporters to the political activities discussed in Chapter 3. In the European Social Survey cited in Figure 3.1 there was a question which asked respondents to indicate if they felt close to a political party; some 48 per cent of the British respondents in this survey indicated that they did feel close. In effect this measured partisanship in the electorate. The question was then followed up by asking respondents how close they were to that party. Altogether 31 per cent of the respondents stated that they were very close or quite close to that party. Therefore, just under a third of the British electorate can be described as reasonably strong party identifiers using this measure. It is interesting to work out the contribution of this minority of partisans to the different types of political participation discussed in Figure 3.1.

Table 4.5 examines the contribution of British partisans to the types of political participation discussed in Chapter 3. It is noteworthy that with one single exception, they were over-represented in all categories of participation in comparison with their numbers in the electorate. For example, partisans made up 31 per cent of the electorate, but 39 per cent of people who voted. This confirms the findings from Chapter 3. But in addition to voting they were also more likely to get involved in boycotting and buying goods for political reasons. They were far more likely to contact politicians and to volunteer in charitable organizations. Both of these types of participation are central to the accountability of government and to the effectiveness of the welfare state. In addition they were very much more likely to donate money to political organi-

Table 4.5   The contribution of individuals to civic engagement, who were close to a political party

Percentages of individuals who were close to a political party	%
In the electorate	31.2
Took part in a protest demonstration	30.8
Who signed a petition	36.9
Voted in the general election	38.5
Boycotted products for political reasons	39.5
Bought products for political reasons	39.9
Contacted politicians or officials	41.1
Volunteered	42.2
Donated money to a political organization	46.2
Wore a badge or sticker	51.0
Worked in a political party	52.9

Source: European Social Survey, 2002, see http://www.europeansocialsurvey.org/.

zations, including political parties, which is vitally important for sustaining democratic politics. They played a very important role in campaigning as measured by their willingness to wear a campaign badge or a sticker. Finally, and not surprisingly they were very important in sustaining parties by working for them at the local level. It is easy to see that if British citizens no longer identified with political parties, there would be a dramatic drop in all types of political participation.

Table 4.5 examines reasonably strong partisans in the electorate. But what of the party members and activists who have been discussed earlier in this chapter? Table 4.6 repeats the analysis of Table 4.5 but this time looking only at party members and active volunteers. Unlike partisans, they make up a small proportion of the British electorate with only 3.5 per cent of respondents indicating that they were either members or had done some voluntary work for a party in the previous year. Despite this, their contribution to political participation in Britain is considerable. They are over-represented in all of the types of political participation examined in Figure 3.1. For example, they were twice as likely to get involved in consumer participation as their numbers in the electorate would imply; they were three times more likely to contact politicians and public officials and to volunteer in the community; they were four times more likely to campaign; and, finally they were a staggering ten times more likely to donate money to political organizations and to work in a political party. The party members are only a small minority of the electorate but they are extremely effective when it comes to supporting political participation in Britain.

Table 4.6   The contribution of party members and active supporters to civic engagement

Percentages of party members and active supporters	%
In the electorate	3.5
Who signed a petition	5.5
Bought products for political reasons	6.6
Boycotted products for political reasons	6.7
Took part in a protest demonstration	7.7
Discuss politics every day	8.0
Contacted a politicians or official	9.4
Who volunteered	10.1
Wore a badge or sticker	12.4
Donated money to a political organisation	24.5
Worked in a political party	26.5

Source: European Social Survey, 2002, see http://www.europeansocialsurvey.org/.

Tables 4.5 and 4.6 examine the role of party supporters and members in sustaining political participation in Britain, but there is also the role of partisans in acting as 'ambassadors in the community' (Scarrow, 1996), that is, debating and communicating politics within the community as a whole. One way of assessing this is by looking at the extent to which strong party supporters and party members contribute to the day-to-day discussion of politics in the country. The European Social Survey shows that while strong party supporters make up 31 per cent of the electorate, they represent 45 per cent of the people who discuss politics every day and about 40 per cent of those who discuss it several times a week. A similar picture emerges in relation to party members and the discussion of politics at the grassroots level. As we saw earlier, they make up only 3.5 per cent of the electorate, yet they constitute 8 per cent of the people who discuss politics every day and just over 5 per cent of those who discuss politics several times a week.

This evidence suggests that strong party supporters and party members play a disproportionate role in sustaining politics and political participation at the grassroots level in Britain. This helps to support civil society since, in their absence, rates of participation would be much lower. Part of this activity is in supporting the daily discourse about politics and government which sustains the political culture of Britain.

The findings have a somewhat disturbing implication, namely that the decline in the strength of partisanship and in party membership discussed earlier in this chapter is very likely to weaken all forms of political participation and, in addition, reduce political communication and the daily discourse surrounding political issues, which takes place in the homes, workplaces and leisure centres of British society. As partisanship weakens and party membership shrinks further this will inhibit other diverse forms of participation, such as boycotting goods, signing petitions and volunteering in the community.

As the earlier discussion indicated, there is a third level at which parties exist, and that is in Parliament. This is the most important level for governance in general and so we consider that next.

Parties at the centre

The primary role of political parties in Parliament in Britain is to provide coherence to government at the centre, as the earlier discussion indicated. Ironically, one of the most interesting trends in government, to set alongside the decline in the strength of partisanship described in Figure 4.1, is that party cohesion has become more and more important to governance over time. This is because government at the centre is trying to do more and more by passing increasing volumes of legislation over time. Figure 4.3 charts the growth in legislation since the Second World War. It includes all primary legislation in the Westminster Parliament and in the Scottish, Welsh and North Ireland Assemblies. It shows that there has been a tremendous increase in such legislation over time.

It is easy to see why successive governments might need to legislate more to cope with the growing complexities of modern society. Policy making involves an ever more complex system of coordination between different organizations and issue communities both within and outside the state (Whiteley, 1986; Smith, 1999). The European and international dimensions of governance have grown successively more important (Bache and George, 2006). Devolution has added to these complexities (Deacon, 2006), as has the need to regulate more closely society and the economy (Sherman, 2008). The state is attempting to do so much more than it would ever have done in previous eras.

Alongside the traditional tasks of maintaining public order, providing defence and investing in infrastructure, the state is increasingly attempting to change behaviour. It is aiming to make people healthier by persuading them to give up smoking and get more exercise; it is seeking to deal with family breakdown and growing welfare needs in society; it is attempting to prevent anti-social behaviour on the part of teenagers, and it faces the redistributive consequences of an ageing society and an increasing ratio of dependents to producers this has brought about

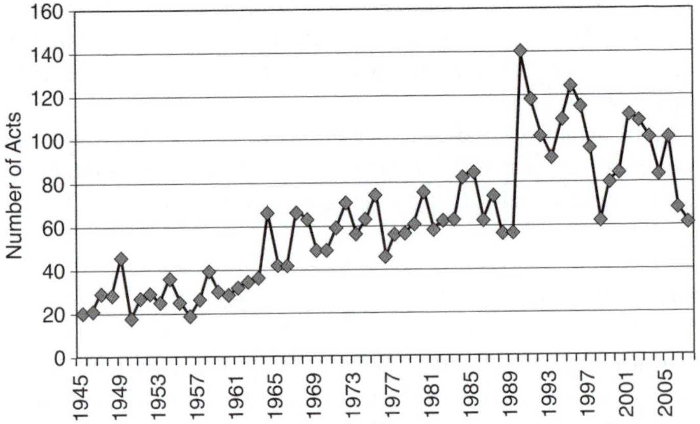

Source: UK Statute Law Database, Office of Public Sector Information; see http://legislation.gov.uk.

Figure 4.3 The number of primary Acts of Parliament, 1945–2008

(Castles, 2007). It is even attempting to influence levels of happiness in society (Whiteley, Clarke, Sanders, Stewart, 2010). Faced with these kinds of challenges it is not surprising that government has become ever more complex and more interventionist over time.

One relatively unnoticed feature of this growing pattern of legislative activity is the need for greater party loyalty to get legislation through Parliament. There has been a trend growth in the number of Parliamentary Divisions, or votes on legislation, in the House of Commons over the post-war period. This is the consequence of the growing legislative agenda in Parliament. Despite the huge policy changes introduced by the post-war Labour government, the average number of Divisions in the House Commons fluctuated at around 200 per year from 1945 to 1951. Moreover, it stayed at that level during the Conservative governments of the 1950s. But by the time of Labour's second post-war term in the 1960s, the number of Divisions had risen to around 300 per year, but with large fluctuations over time. The average number of Divisions per year has stayed quite close to that figure subsequently, but it is noticeable that the fluctuations have been reduced. Whereas in the 1970s the number of Parliamentary Divisions could easily fall below 100 in a given year, this has never occurred since 1997. Parliamentarians can now regularly expect to face more than 300 Divisions per year, and that number is very unlikely to fall below 200 in any given year. Parliament is legislating more over time and consequently governments have had to rely on the party loyalties of their Members of Parliament to a greater extent to get things through the House of Commons and House of Lords.

This means that governments need greater party loyalty if they are successfully to implement their legislative proposals. But they are drawing on a depleting reservoir of party loyalty in order to do this. There has been a reaction to these developments by Members of Parliament which takes the form of a growth of backbench rebellions in the House of Commons under successive governments. This trend has been well documented (Cowley, 1998, 2002, 2005). To give some illustrative examples, Cowley charts 47 major rebellions in which MPs from all three major parties voted against their own party line in the 2001–5 Parliament. Examples include the 46 Labour MPs who rebelled over the issue of faith schools in February 2002; 72 Labour backbenchers who opposed the second reading of the Higher Education Bill in December 2003, which introduced university top-up fees. However, the largest rebellion to take place in the House since the nineteenth-century passage of the Corn Laws, occurred in March 2003. A total of 139 Labour MPs supported an amendment by Chris Smith, a former minister in the government, stating that the case for military action against Iraq was 'unproven'. Sixteen Conservative MPs also defied their Whips on the same vote.

In his discussion of the reasons for Parliamentary loyalty, Cowley makes the point that a norm of party loyalty is quite strong in the House of Commons. He writes:

By the time someone becomes an MP they will have been a member of their party for years, usually decades....Those who become MPs will have been amongst the most active members of their party. By the time they reach Westminster they'll have put in hours, days, weeks of unpaid work on behalf of the party... This leaves a mark. It means that for most MPs, going against their party is not an easy thing to do. It is rarely done lightly. (Cowley, 2005: 25)

The important point is that the party loyalty, which holds the system together, was acquired and reinforced among the grassroots party activists, not in the House of Commons. If the grassroots party organization all but disappears and partisanship in the electorate weakens to the point that it is marginal to the electoral process, this is likely to have major consequences for the norms of loyalty identified in Cowley's analysis. In these circumstances, party loyalty in the House of Commons is likely to weaken to the point that rebellion becomes as common place as it is in the US House of Representatives (Sundquist, 1981).

Relatively weak parties in the US Congress have been a feature of American politics for many years. They are a problem for governance in the United States, but the Executive President continues to govern, even when the legislature is in disarray. This state of affairs is not possible under the Westminster system where the executive is directly dependent on party loyalty in the House of Commons. It is very difficult to see how British government could operate in a world of weak partisan attachments in the House of Commons comparable to those in the US Congress.

The culmination of these processes can be seen with the Coalition government of the Conservatives and Liberal Democrats that occured after the inconclusive general election of 2010. This general election was inconclusive partly because partisanship had weakened among the voters to the point where there was insufficient support for the major parties to bring about a decisive result, and electors were willing to abstain or vote for minor parties in increasing numbers. This lack of party cohesion has subsequently fed through into the House of Commons, which has become more rebellious under the Coalition government than under the previous Labour administration. Thus the weakening of partisanship is beginning to influence the effectiveness of government itself, a topic that is discussed more fully in Chapter 8.

Conclusion

This chapter has explained why political parties are so central to governance and to politics in Britain, and has drawn attention to the trends which serve to undermine the cohesion of parties and governments in the long run. We have governments elected by relatively small minorities of citizens attempting to act as if they have a strong mandate to govern. We have trend increases in the volume of legislation and in the instruments of government at the centre, which reflect the growing complexities of society and the state, but a depleting stock of 'political capital' on which they need to draw if they are to govern. At some point these trends will reach a crisis, with electoral volatility rising to new heights, and partisanship weakening to the point that it only plays a relatively minor role in electoral politics.

The first clear signs of a major shift occurred in the 2010 general election in which no party could achieve an overall majority, and so a formal coalition was formed between the Conservatives and Liberal Democrats.

At the time of writing it is not clear how long this coalition can hold together given the huge cuts in public expenditure on which it is embarking, following the financial crises of 2008–9. Needless to say if maintaining party loyalty in the House of Commons is increasingly difficult within one party, it is not surprising that it is more difficult with two parties (see http://www.revolts.co.uk). Moreover the problems for the Coalition government are likely to increase as it tries to impose unprecedented cuts on the public sector in response to the financial crisis. This means that there is a real question mark about whether or not the government has the political capital to force through such unpopular policies.

At some point governments in the future will have to consider root-and-branch reform of the party system if it is not to become ineffective. We will return to these issues and to the question of constitutional reform in Chapter 9. But for the moment, this chapter has examined an important but rather narrow aspect of voluntary activity in Britain, namely political parties. But this raises wider issues of the extent to which voluntary activity in general is in decline in Britain, and that is the topic of the next chapter.

5

Voluntary Activity and Social Capital

Chapter 4 focused on political parties, which are one type of voluntary organization, and, consequently, in this chapter we widen the focus to look at voluntary activity more generally. It is fair to say that volunteering has always been recognized as an important feature of civil society in Britain (see Almond and Verba, 1963). But work over the last ten years or so has shown that it is even more important than the earlier research suggested, because of its contribution to social capital. The concept of social capital has become more and more influential in social science in recent years. As Chapter 3 explained, social capital refers to cooperative relationships between individuals based on mutual trust and norms of reciprocation. Students of social capital look at networks of volunteering, the effectiveness of voluntary activity and interpersonal trust in society. It transpires that unpaid voluntary activities make a very important contribution to social capital, which, in turn, has all kinds of benign effects on society and politics, and therefore, trends in volunteering take on a particular significance for supporting civil society (see Putnam, 1993, 2000).

As we mentioned earlier, the core idea of social capital is that individuals who learn to trust each other and to work together to solve common social problems, can have a big impact on society. High levels of social capital have been linked to improved health, better educational standards, lower crime rates, enhanced political participation, and improved economic performance (see the review in Halpern, 2005). Overall, this research suggests that social capital is a very desirable thing for society and can do much to improve the everyday lives of citizens as well as make government more effective.

Voluntary activity, trust and social capital

As the earlier discussion indicated, the sociologist James Coleman introduced the term social capital into modern social theory (Coleman, 1990). He defined it as a set of obligations and expectations, which operate between individuals and also as a set of information channels linking people within networks of engagement. At its broadest, social interactions generate 'credit slips' of obligations and norms of recipro- cation, and where these norms are strong they can be utilized by every- one in society to solve social problems. For example, if an individual accidentally leaves their wallet on the train it is likely to be returned to them intact in a society where social capital is high, because citizens in such a society trust each other and feel a strong sense of obligation to help each other out. They are likely to feel empathy towards someone who faces this predicament and want to help.

On the other hand, in societies where social capital is weak, individ- uals tend to distrust each other and the missing item is most unlikely to turn up intact. In this case people feel little empathy for each other and, since they expect to be cheated by strangers, they have little compunc- tion in taking advantage of others. Social capital is like any other types of capital in the sense that it can be put to use to make society more pro- ductive and efficient. Just as financial capital can be invested in order to stimulate economic growth, and human capital, or education, can be used to raise productivity, social capital can be used to achieve similar objectives (Whiteley, 2000).

For most writers interpersonal trust is the key indicator of social capital (Putnam, 1993; Fukuyama, 1995; Van Deth *et al.*, 1999). Trust is important because it allows individuals to move beyond their own immediate family or community and engage in cooperative behaviour with strangers. Trusting relationships within the family, the immediate community or ethnic group have been referred to as 'bonding' social capital – divided societies can have a great deal of this type of social capital since it does not generally move across ethnic, linguistic or geo- graphical barriers (Putnam, 1993). In this situation people trust members of the 'in group' and distrust everyone else. On the other hand 'bridging' social capital which does cross such barriers serves to bring different groups together and consequently is much more important.

There is a debate about the origins of social capital, and its causes have been linked to many factors such as levels of inequality in society, educational attainment, ethnic divisions, age differences, family rela- tionships, social class, and even the amount of television watched in a society (Halpern, 2005, ch. 8). Many factors are involved and they operate at the individual, local and national levels. If an individual is a reliable person then their fellow citizens tend to trust them, and if the community in which they live is also a trusting one everyone can trans- act business with a handshake. In addition, if a society also has high levels of trust, when someone from travels to a strange city they will expect to be treated fairly by its inhabitants, and in turn they will be inclined to treat others fairly as well.

High levels of trust help to save on what economists call transaction costs – the price people pay for doing business. In a trusting society, these costs are likely to be small, since if people give their word that they will do something then generally they can be expected to deliver on that promise. There is no need to draw up elaborate contracts and have lawyers standing by to enforce bargains. In a non-trusting society, however, things are different and enforcement mechanisms such as formal contracts, lawyers and the courts are required to ensure compliance, and these all increase the costs of doing business.

One influential explanation of the origins of social capital was introduced by Alexis de Tocqueville, the French philosopher who studied American society in the early nineteenth century (De Tocqueville, 1990). Writing in 1832, de Tocqueville commented on the widespread growth of voluntary organizations in American society. In his view, what we now describe as social capital, originates in face-to-face interactions between individuals within voluntary associations. By working together in a voluntary setting individuals learn cooperative skills and also acquire the willingness to trust others, which is central to social capital. The key relationships involve voluntary interactions rather than market interactions, as these are not motivated by monetary gain.

Putnam's study of Italy precipitated much of the contemporary interest in social capital. He explained social and economic differences between the Italian regions, and in a later book, between American states, in terms of their different endowments of social capital (1993, 2000). He found that in areas such as Minnesota or Emilia-Romagna, people were socially active – they joined groups and took part in a wide variety of voluntary associations, both formal and informal, which put them in close contact with their fellow citizens. This activity served to build a reservoir of social capital in these communities and helped to develop 'norms of reciprocity'. People came to expect fair dealing both from their fellows and also from strangers. By contrast, in places such as Mississippi or Calabria, civic life did not appear to be conducive to building social capital. In these places, associational life was relatively weak, norms of reciprocity limited and levels of interpersonal trust low.

The theory suggests that interpersonal trust and voluntary activity are linked together in a virtuous circle, so that as people interact in a voluntary setting, they come to know and trust each other and this, in turn, promotes even more voluntary activity. As a consequence, those feelings of trust begin to extend to people beyond an individual's immediate circle of acquaintances. These interactions produce what the economists call 'externalities', which arise when cooperative behaviour spills over into the wider society. Because they know and trust their fellow citizens, individuals are more likely to trust and to help strangers. As social capital develops, society works more efficiently by reducing the trans-action and policing costs which arise when there is widespread mistrust between individuals. Societies poor in social capital display only weak associational ties and exhibit limited mutual trust, and as a result, they fare worse and work less efficiently than their more fortunate neighbours.

It is important to note that voluntary activity is much broader concept than political participation. In Putnam's interpretation, social capital can be built in all types of voluntary organizations such as sports clubs, cultural organizations, choral societies, as well as in informal groups such as pub darts teams or reading groups, none of which have much to do with political participation. However, it is also true that voluntary activity in political organizations is a type of social capital, but it is much narrower than social capital in general. The social capital model argues that these relatively non-political forms of voluntary activity are the building blocks of civil society and can stimulate political participation by building trust between individuals.

We mentioned earlier that social capital appears to have major consequences for society. Empirical research suggests that societies in which social capital is high perform much better on a range of economic and political indicators than societies which lack social capital (Knack and Keefer, 1997; Inglehart, 1999; Whiteley, 2000; Newton and Norris, 2000; Knack, 2002). Putnam claims that social capital in America delivers many benefits to the localities where it is strong, including higher economic growth, improved health and education, reduced crime and even higher levels of happiness (Putnam, 2000).

But social capital may not be an infinitely renewable resource. There is evidence of a decline in social capital in the United States since the 1960s: in an influential argument, Putnam blames television for this development (Putnam, 1995, 2000). Television now constitutes the main leisure pursuit for very large numbers of westerners. The trend towards television watching grew rapidly in the 1950s in Britain and the United States, and it serves to isolate people in their own homes, and reduce the time they have available for precisely the various kinds of social networking and associational activity which are conducive to developing social capital. This claim is controversial, however, and has been challenged (Norris, 1996).

Social capital theory has been subject to considerable critical scrutiny, both of a theoretical and an empirical nature (Tarrow, 1996; Newton, 1999; Claibourn and Martin, 2000; Milner, 2002; Halpern, 2005). One line of criticism is that the concept has become vague since it has been applied rather indiscriminately to many different social phenomena. Lin and Erickson (2010) point out that various definitions of social capital have included:

> network features (strength of ties, density), social relations (parent–child, parent–teacher, number of friends or peers, influence of friends or peers), frequency of interactions, perceived relations or support, as well as generalized or interpersonal trust, cohesion, reciprocity and so forth. (2010: 2)

They make the sensible suggestion that the definition should be sharpened and narrowed if it is to be scientifically useful. In a sense, the proliferation of meanings attached to the term is an indicator of its success in providing theoretical insights into many social phenomena. We will avoid this problem by adhering fairly closely to the original definition by Coleman and Putnam who both emphasize the importance of interpersonal trust and networks of civic engagement.

Another critical debate in the social capital literature relates to whether it is a purely aggregate phenomenon, that is, a characteristic of groups and societies, or whether it is primarily an individual level phenomenon. Kawachi and Berkman (2000) argue that analysis of social capital should be reserved exclusively for the study of groups by means of what is known as ecological analysis. The argument given is that it is a property of collectives and cannot be understood purely in terms of individuals. As can often happen, other researchers take the opposite view, with Portes (1998) concluding that 'the greatest theoretical promise of social capital lies at the individual level' (1998: 21). In fact, social capital can be productively studied both at the individual and collective levels. It is manifest in the former by the willingness of individuals to trust others and to get involved in voluntary activities and in the latter by the vibrancy of communities and the strength of their civic engagement. There is no need to arbitrarily confine it to one level of analysis.

Finally, it has been argued that social capital researchers are too inclined to emphasize the benefits and rather too willing to ignore the problems of social capital (Edwards and Foley, 1998). It can be argued that bonding forms of social capital, in particular, exclude people, giving

rise to discrimination and social inequality rather than trust and coop-
eration. This point can be illustrated by the case of Northern Ireland;
there was plenty of social capital within the Nationalist and the Unionist
communities in this province at the height of the troubles, the problem
was that it failed to travel between these communities. This is a fair
point, but it has not been ignored in the early work on social capital,
particularly by Putnam who wrote about the 'dark side' of social capital
(2000: ch. 22).

One early finding, which attracted a lot of attention, was that while
social capital appears to have been declining in the United States, it does
not appear to have declined very much in Britain (Hall, 1999). However,
Hall's work studied trends only up to the early 1990s, and subsequent
work suggests that since then social capital has declined in Britain in a
rather similar way to the US (Grenier and Wright, 2001). This is obvi-
ously an important question which will be examined more fully below.

In relation to the research on the effects of social capital in Britain,
another finding is that in studies of local government service delivery,
outputs are not influenced by social capital, but service outcomes are.
Outputs refer to the amount of money spent by local authorities on the
delivery of education and welfare services, while outcomes refer to the
effectiveness of those services at the point of delivery. In other words
outputs come before outcomes. In the case of education, which is the
biggest item in the budget for English and Welsh local authorities, the
best pupil performances in GCSE are found in areas with high levels of
associational activity. At the same time there is no clear relationship
between associational activity and local spending on education (Pattie,
Seyd and Whiteley, 2004: 189–223). This indicates that there are other
factors which explain effective policy delivery other than spending, and
these are related to social capital. There are similar studies in the United
States, for example in relation to real-estate development and urban
management schemes; it appears that social capital significantly
improves the quality of policy delivery in these schemes (Saegert and
Winkel, 1998; Glaeser and Sacerdote, 2000).

These findings all suggest that social capital is an asset to good governance, but its relationship to political participation is more ambiguous.
Putnam (2000: 31–64) produced a great deal of evidence to support the
idea that social capital and political participation have both declined at
the same time in the United States. Moreover, individual level analyses
of civic participation repeatedly show a correlation between personal
affluence and education on the one hand, and indicators of social capital
such as trust and voluntary activity on the other (Parry, Moyser and Day,

1992; Brady, Verba and Schlozman, 1995; Franklin, 2004). It is well known that community affluence and levels of education are determinants of political participation so if these are driven, in part, by social capital, this establishes an important indirect link between social capital and participation.

On the other hand, as Eric Oliver (2001) points out, social capital is not the same thing as affluence and other, subtler, relationships are possible. He suggests that participation varies systematically across different types of American suburban communities. Even after controlling for individual-level factors such as personal affluence, political participation is greater, *ceteris paribus*, in economically mixed communities than in very poor or very rich communities. It is also greater in racially mixed than in near all-black or all-white communities. Both reflect the greater political stakes in 'mixed' rather than in homogenous communities. Politics in diverse communities involve a battle between potential 'winners' and 'losers', whereas in homogenous communities residents have rather similar interests, and hence the risks of non-participation and the potential gains from participation are not so great. In homogenous communities people can leave it to their neighbours to protect their interests because these neighbours are very much like themselves. In heterogeneous communities they have to get involved if they want policies to be delivered that protect their interests. This point is a challenge to social capital theory, since it is often the most homogenous communities which have the most social capital.

Another important factor in explaining political participation is the size of the communities in which people live. Those living in less populous communities are more likely, other things being equal, to participate than people living in larger urban centres (Oliver, 2000; Frandsen, 2002). This, it is claimed, reflects the relatively smaller prospects of people free-riding in small communities than in a large one. In small towns where people tend to know each other such free-riding is likely to be frowned on and not socially sanctioned. In contrast, in more anonymous conurbations social sanctions are much weaker and so allow free-riding. Equally, the evidence suggests that more people trust local government in smaller communities than in large urban conurbations (Denters, 2002). Again these findings are inconsistent with the social capital model, which suggests that there is no necessary relationship between the size of a community and levels of social capital.

An important problem associated with research into social capital is establishing the causal processes at work. Does social capital explain participation, or is it the other way round? There may be virtuous or vicious circles at work in these relationships, but unless the starting point of the interaction can be identified, social capital runs the risk of being a theory without any solid foundations. To be fair, given that voluntary activity is a much broader concept than political participation it is not tautological to argue that voluntary activity drives political participation.

In light of this discussion, we are left with two key questions. First, is there evidence to suggest that social capital in Britain is declining over time? Or is it fairly stable as Hall (1999) suggested in his influential article? The second and subsequent question relates to the impact of social capital on civic engagement and norms of reciprocation. How relevant is social capital to civil society? Is a decline in social capital in Britain associated with a decline in civic engagement and in the norms which support civil society? We address these issues next.

Changes in social capital and voluntary activity in Britain

Given the importance of social capital and voluntary activity for effective governance and policy making, the question of the decline in social capital in Britain takes on considerable significance. As always, there are difficulties in getting adequate data to measure trends over time, and certainly the British data is nowhere near as rich as in the United States. However, there are some indications that suggest that social capital is declining in Britain. The decline in voluntary party activity discussed in Chapter 4 is one indicator, since this is a special type of social capital. In addition, there has also been a large decline in trade union membership, which peaked at just over 13 million members in 1979 and was down to 6.9 million by 2008 (Barratt, 2008). Church membership has been declining for many years, as have traditional women's organizations such as the Women's Institute (Halpern, 2005: 213). Similarly, evidence from the British Cohort Study suggests that a fairly large decline in membership of voluntary organizations occurred between the age cohorts born immediately after the Second World War and those born in the 1950s and later (Ferri, Bynner and Wadsworth, 2003).

We can investigate this issue in more detail with the help of data from the World Values Surveys. These surveys, which go back to 1981, are primarily designed to chart changes in the values and attitudes of citizens in a large number of countries over time. Their purpose is to investigate the change from materialistic to post-materialist value orientations in affluent societies discussed by Ronald Inglehart (1997). The former

Table 5.1   Membership of voluntary organizations in Britain, 1981–99

Organization	1981 (%)	1990 (%)	1999 (%)
Welfare service for the elderly	8.6	7.1	6.8
Religious organization	21.0	16.6	4.8
Arts, music or cultural organization	8.0	9.3	10.4
Trade union	19.9	14.4	7.3
Political party	4.7	4.9	2.6
Human rights organization	1.5	2.0	2.6
Youth work organization	7.6	4.6	5.5
Local political action group	—	2.7	3.5
Conservation, environmental group	—	5.0	1.5
Sports or recreation group	—	16.9	3.0
Women's group	—	4.8	1.5
Peace movement	—	1.1	0.5
Health organization	—	3.5	3.3

Source: World Values Surveys; see http://www.worldvaluessurvey.org/.

relate to values which stress the importance of personal security and economic welfare, while the latter stress personal autonomy and individual self-fulfilment. The surveys include questions about membership in voluntary organizations and also questions about interpersonal trust, the two touchstone indicators of social capital. It is possible, therefore, to examine changes in these variables over a considerable period of time in Britain.

Table 5.1 shows data on membership of various voluntary organizations in Britain from the 1981 through to 1999 from the World Values Surveys. In the 1990 survey, new questions about membership in additional voluntary organizations were included alongside the ones asked in 1981, and so it is possible to chart changes over 18 years for some organizations and over 9 years for others. It is noteworthy that for the seven types of organization tracked over 18 years, five of them showed declining memberships. There was a large drop in the membership of trade unions and also in religious organizations, and more modest reduction in welfare organizations for the elderly, in political parties and in youth work organizations. The two exceptions were arts and culture organizations and human rights groups, with modest increases in the memberships of both.

Looking at the six organizations, which can be tracked during the 1990s, they all experienced a loss of membership with a single exception. Sports organizations appear to have lost a large number of members as did women's groups and environmental groups. Health-

Table 5.2   Interpersonal trust in Britain, 1981–99

	Most people can be trusted (%)	*You can't be too careful dealing with people (%)*
1981	43.1	56.9
1990	43.7	56.3
1999	29.6	70.4
2005	30.4	69.6

Source: World Values Surveys; see http://www.worldvaluessurvey.org/.

related organizations and peace groups experienced more modest declines, and finally local political action groups appear to have had a modest increase in membership during this period. Taken as a whole, however, the evidence suggests that voluntary organizations in Britain have, with some exceptions, been declining over time. If so, this data would support the suggestion that social capital in Britain has been declining as well during this period.

Another way of addressing the same issue is to examine changes in interpersonal trust, the other important dimension of social capital. This is shown in Table 5.2 which records responses to a question in the World Values Survey, which asked: 'Generally speaking do you think that most people can be trusted, or that you can't be too careful in dealing with people?' In this case it was possible to get data from the 2005 World Values Survey in Britain, and so the series runs for almost a quarter of a century. It shows fairly clearly that interpersonal trust declined a great deal during this period, although the rate of decline was far from uniform. It appears that trust eroded fairly rapidly during the 1990s, but after that period the decline stabilized.

We can get a more nuanced view of changing levels of volunteering and trust with data from the Continuous Monitoring Survey of the British Election Study. This is a monthly series of internet-based surveys that have been running since April 2004 and were discussed in Chapter 2 in relation to the delivery of policies (Clarke, Sanders, Stewart and Whiteley, 2009). Since the decline in social capital is slow, monthly data over a period of a few years is unlikely to pick up large effects. But there are nonetheless discernible trends in the data. Figure 5.1 shows the percentage of people who volunteered in an organization in the previous year. The data covers the period from April 2004 to December 2010, and shows that there were significant fluctuations in the data over time, but an overall slow but discernible decline took place in volunteering

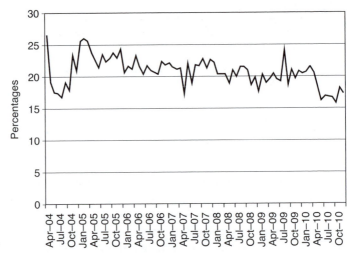

Source: BES, various years; see http://www.data-archive.ac.uk/.

Figure 5.1   Trends in volunteering, April 2004 December 2010

during this period. Setting aside short-term fluctuations, more than 20 per cent of respondents regularly reported volunteering up to the end of 2007, but after then the average figure fell to 20 per cent or less. It is no coincidence that this was the beginning of the worst financial crisis and recession in eighty years, suggesting that the state of the economy has an influence on social capital.

Figure 5.2 repeats the same exercise for a measure of interpersonal trust in the Continuous Monitoring Survey. Trust is measured by means of an eleven-point scale with respondents scoring zero being very reluctant to trust anyone and respondents scoring ten being very trusting. In this case the data fluctuates much more than does the volunteering data in Figure 5.1. It is important to remember that the trust scale is a more fine-grained measure than the volunteering scale and this makes it more likely to pick up short-term fluctuations. Notwithstanding this point, on average the trust score ends up significantly lower at the end of the period than it was at the beginning. Again this could have been influenced by the recession which occurred towards the end of the series. Taken together, these rather different and more frequently measured indicators of trust and volunteering tell a similar story to that of the World Values data.

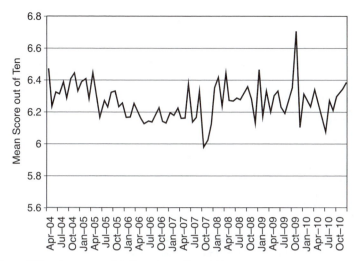

Source: BES, various years; see http://www.data-archive.ac.uk/.

Figure 5.2 Trends in interpersonal trust, April 2004–December 2010

What of the relationship between the two key measures, voluntary activity and interpersonal trust? As the earlier discussion indicated, the social capital literature emphasizes the importance of the links between these two phenomena, and the strength of this relationship can be seen in Table 5.3, again using the World Values data. This replicates the number of groups identified in Table 5.1 but this time compares levels of trust among group members and non-members. Clearly, if voluntary activity interacts with trust we should expect to see a difference between trust levels of the volunteers and those in the rest of the community. It can be seen that in every case levels of trust are higher among members of these voluntary organizations than it is in the general population. Trust is clearly associated with volunteering.

This relationship suggests that there is a link between declining levels of trust and declining levels of voluntary activity in Britain. Social capital is declining partly because people are less trusting but also because they are less willing to volunteer. Moreover, these two variables interact with each other, so as the numbers of volunteers diminish there should be a decline in levels of trust in society. Whether declining trust produces less volunteering or the process works in reverse is less important than the fact that these appear to be working together. Given this,

Table 5.3   The relationship between trust and voluntary activity

Organization	Percentage who trust and are members of an organization	Percentage who trust and are not members
Welfare service for the elderly	48.8	38.7
Religious organization	49.5	37.7
Arts, music or cultural organization	57.9	37.6
Trade union	47.8	38.1
Political party	63.1	38.4
Human rights organization	66.7	38.9
Youth work organization	53.2	38.6
Local political action group	54.3	37.3
Conservation, environmental group	56.3	35.9
Sports or recreation group	51.1	36.0
Women's group	55.4	37.1
Peace movement	65.0	37.5
Health organization	51.3	37.3

Source: World Values Surveys; see http://www.worldvaluessurvey.org/.

it is important to understand the consequences of this development for British society and this will be examined next.

The consequences of declining social capital

In earlier chapters we examined the norms and beliefs that underpin citizenship in Britain, together with and analysis of trends in political participation. Since we have established in this chapter that social capital is declining over time, it is interesting to examine the relationship between these norms and diverse forms of participation and indicators of social capital. If beliefs about what it takes to be a good citizen are related to measures of social capital such as interpersonal trust, then it follows that a decline in trust is likely to produce a weakening of such norms. Similarly, if voluntary activity is associated with political participation, then the decline in the membership of voluntary organizations described in the earlier tables implies a decline in political participation as well.

We start the examination of the relationship between trust and citizenship by looking at some of the attitudes described in Chapter 2. It will be recalled that in that chapter we discussed the priorities of someone who aspired to be a good citizen. If we revisit that data it is readily apparent that individuals who are trusting attached a higher priority to the various characteristics of the good citizen than the non-trusting. Thus 84 per cent of the trusting think that voting is very important compared with 78 per cent of the non-trusting; 80 per cent of the trusting think that it is important to understand the opinions of others compared with 72 per cent of the non-trusting; finally, 66 per cent of the trusting think it is important to help the under-privileged compared with 62 per cent of the non-trusting.

There are two exceptions to this pattern which relate to the importance of not evading taxes, where there is no difference between the two, and a willingness to serve in the military. In the latter case, the non-trusting are more likely to think that military service is important than the trusting. The differences between the trusting and the non-trusting are not very large, but there is a consistent pattern in the data, with people who are trusting have stronger norms about what the good citizen should do than people who are not trusting. This evidence suggests that trust helps to support the norms which underpin citizenship in Britain. By implication, if interpersonal trust declines over time, then it is likely that such norms will weaken at the same time.

In addition to norms about citizenship another important aspect of attitudes discussed in Chapter 2 was tolerance of other people's views. It will be recalled that respondents were asked if they would be in favour of allowing public meetings by religious extremists, revolutionaries and racists. The percentages of trusting and non-trusting respondents who said such meetings should definitely be allowed again differed. In this case the picture is mixed, since the trusting respondents were significantly more tolerant of religious extremists and revolutionaries than their non-trusting counterparts. However, the reverse was true in the case of racists where the trusting were more intolerant than the non-trusting. This undoubtedly reflects the fact that there are limits to tolerance if the groups involved appear to be a threat to society. Overall however, this suggests that a long-term decline in trust in society could have adverse consequences for tolerance of minorities.

Another issue examined in Chapter 2 was political efficacy. It was argued that citizens need a sense of efficacy – a belief that they can make a difference – if they are to participate in politics. If we look at the relationship between trust and efficacy, it is apparent that the trusting are more likely to say that they have influence on the government than the non-trusting. For example, just over four out of ten people who are trusting agreed with the statement: 'People like me don't have any say about what government does'. In contrast, about half of the people who are not trusting agree with the same statement. A similar pattern emerged in relation to the statement: 'I don't think the government cares much what people like me think'. Half of the people who are trusting agreed with the statement compared with close to two thirds of people who are not trusting. It is apparent, therefore, that there is an association between trust and efficacy. The latter is important because it is one of the key ingredients of political action. People are more likely to get involved if they think that they can make a difference. Clearly a long-term decline in levels of trust in society is likely to have the effect of undermining efficacy and thus participation.

Turning next to interest in politics, this was discussed in Chapter 2 as an important contributory factor in explaining political participation. Once again, there is a relationship between trust and interest in politics in the Citizenship Survey. Thus 45 per cent of people who are trusting said that they were fairly interested in politics, compared with only 37 per cent of the non-trusting. At the other end of the scale about one-third of people who are trusting said that they were not very interested in politics compared with just under 40 per cent of the non-trusting. Trust and interest in politics are clearly related to each other. It seems likely that a long-term decline in trust will have adverse consequences on the level of interest in politics in the future.

In Chapter 2, we briefly examined the extent to which people trust the government, which is an important component of the civic culture. In what is now becoming a familiar pattern, there is a relationship between trusting other people and trusting the government. Just over a third of people who trust others agree with the statement: 'people in the government generally try to do what is right', compared with just under a quarter of the non-trusting. Given that trust in other people is associated with trust in government, it seems likely that a long-term decline in interpersonal trust will also have the effect of undermining trust in government.

Up to this point we have been examining the relationship between trust and norms and attitudes of various kinds. The earlier discussion highlights the importance of the relationship between such norms and political participation, thus in Figure 5.3 we examine the association between trust and participation. The figure repeats the analysis of Chapter 3 by examining the percentage of respondents in the Citizenship Survey who participated in various political activities in the previous year. Once again, they are divided into the trusting and the non-trusting. In each case the trusting are more likely to participate in politics than the non-trusting, and this is true for every type of activity. The gap between the trusting and non-trusting is wide for signing a petition,

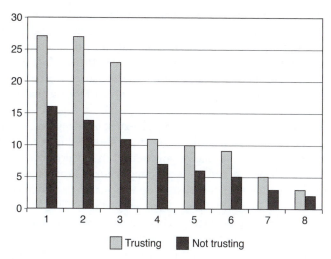

Note:
1. Sign a petition;
2. Donate money or raise funds for a political activity;
3. Boycott products;
4. Attend a political meeting;
5. Contact a politician;
6. Take part in a demonstration;
7. Contact the media;
8. Join an internet political forum.

(Interpersonal trust was recorded from a four-point scale in the surveys where 1 and 2 count as trusting and 3 and 4 count as not trusting.)

Source: ISSP, *Citizenship Survey, 2004* (N=833).

Figure 5.3   The relationship between trust and political participation

donating money to a political cause or boycotting goods for political reasons. The discussion in Chapter 3 indicated that boycotting or consumer participation in particular was growing more important over time, but the implication of these findings is that this growth may slow down or reverse itself if levels of interpersonal trust continue to decline. Similar points can be made about contacting the media and donating money to political causes, the differences between the trusting and the non-trusting are particularly marked.

When it comes to more traditional activities such as signing a petition, going on a protest march or attending a political meeting, the gap between the trusting and the non-trusting is narrower, although it is still apparent. The gap between the trusting and the non-trusting is really narrow for contacting the media and joining an internet political forum. In fact one of the reasons for this is technical rather than substantive in that such activities are still comparatively rare in Britain. If few people do something, then it is difficult for a significant gap to open up between any groups in relation to their participation, not just the trusting and the non-trusting.

Finally, it is interesting to examine the extent to which trust changes people's perceptions of the role of government. It will be recalled that public perceptions of the role of government in modern society were explored in Chapter 2, and it appears that there is strong support for government to intervene in society to do things such as provide health care for the sick, to protect the environment and provide a decent standard of living for elderly citizens. There is less support for things, such as providing a job for anyone who wants one or making affordable housing available. Does trust influence perceptions of the role of government in our society?

Once again the data suggests that it does, with the trusting more likely to favour intervention in the economy and society than those who are not trusting. The biggest gap between the views of these two groups is in relation to environmental protection. The trusting are much more likely to favour government intervention to protect the environment than the non-trusting. Generally, the pattern appears to be that the gap between the trusting and non-trusting is wider for the really popular policies, such as providing health care and a decent standard of living for the elderly, than for the less popular policies, for instance, providing a job for everyone who wants one or maintaining adequate benefits for the unemployed. For the most popular item, healthcare, the gap between the trusting and non-trusting is 11 per cent, but for the least popular item, supporting the unemployed, it is only 2 per cent. It appears that if citizens in general have misgivings about the effectiveness of government in relation to job creation or helping the unemployed, then there is not much of a difference between the trusting and the non-trusting with respect to these policies.

Conclusion

This chapter has demonstrated two important points. First, social capital in Britain, as measured by interpersonal trust and voluntary activity appears to be declining over time. The same trends are apparent in

Britain as those tracked by Robert Putnam in the United States (2000). The second is that social capital is related to many other indicators of the civic culture, including citizenship norms, tolerance, efficacy, interest in politics and political participation. This cumulative pattern of evidence suggests that civil society will be weakened further in the future if the decline of interpersonal trust and volunteering continues. We will examine what can be done about this in a later chapter, but for the moment it is clear that the civic foundations of British democracy are eroding and this problem needs to be addressed if British democracy is to be sustained.

This completes the analysis of the role of voluntary organizations and voluntary activity in encouraging civic engagement. In the next chapter we go on to consider the effects of another group of key organizations in British society – the media. The focus is on the role of the media in promoting or inhibiting the civic culture in Britain.

6

The Media and Political Participation in Britain

The media play a key role in the political life of a modern democracy, such as Britain, for the reason that most political information acquired by citizens comes from the media, as against their direct experience of the political process. In an election campaign, for example, some of the information they receive about the election will come from discussions with friends and family, but much of it will come from the media, that is, television, radio and the newspapers. Thus a great deal of the political information received by citizens is mediated by others rather than being the product of their direct experience. Increasingly, 'impersonal influence' that derives from anonymous 'others', who are not known to the person concerned, shapes political views (Mutz, 1998). The media are the key conduit for these impersonal 'others' by providing news, political analysis, and explaining trends in public opinion over time. These mediating agencies analyse and interpret events in a way which helps citizens make sense of the political world.

The purpose of this chapter is to examine the ways in which citizens use the media in Britain to acquire political information, and also to explore the extent to which the media can influence opinions. Part of this task is to examine the mechanisms by which the media can influence citizen attitudes and behaviour. A key issue is whether or not the media can turn people off politics, because for much of the time it tends to focus on the negative rather than on the positive. Bad news tends to sell more newspapers than good news, and this can produce a 'media malaise', arising from the negative bias in stories about politics and government. The media emphasize conflicts, scandals, and disasters with the result that people become fearful and anxious about the world of politics to the point where they lose interest and won't participate.

We begin the discussion by looking at the extent to which Britons are media consumers, and in particular the extent to which they rely on the media for political information.

Media usage in Britain

The starting point of any analysis of the effects of the media in Britain is to examine the amount of time citizens spend consuming different types of media. The European Social Surveys have some media usage questions in their questionnaires and so it is possible to build up a picture of media usage in Britain from these surveys. Respondents in the 2008 survey were asked questions about the amount of time they spent watching television, listening to the radio or reading newspapers during the average weekday. The responses in the British data in the 2008 survey appear in Table 6.1. In the case of television very few people reported watching no television at all, and the most common category was those who reported watching between one and two hours of television a day. Just over a fifth of respondents said that they watched more than three hours of television a day.

In the survey a lot more people claimed never to listen to the radio than was true of watching television, with just over a quarter of respondents in this category. Again about a fifth of respondents stated that they listened to the radio for more than three hours a day, a similar picture to that of television. For radio, the most popular category was listening for up to an hour a day. When mass television audiences first arrived in Britain in the 1950s it was widely predicted that radio would be eclipsed and television would completely replace it, but clearly this has not happened in practice.

Newspaper readership was the least used media of the three with 30 per cent of respondents saying that they never read a newspaper. Not surprisingly very few people spent more than two hours a day reading newspapers and the largest group of just under 60 per cent spent just less than an hour reading a paper. Newspaper readership has been falling in recent years, whereas this is not true of television and radio, so the press faces the most uncertain economic future at the present time. However, there is a great deal of media consumption in Britain with television leading the way as the most popular medium in the country.

One of the reasons why newspaper readership is falling is the growth of the internet, which is rapidly taking over as a key source of information for most Britons. The 2008 European Social Survey included a question about internet usage which showed that around 70 per cent of Britons reported being users in 2008 with around 30 per cent reporting that they had no access, or that they never used the internet. Of those who reported using the internet some 61 per cent said that they logged on every day and a further 22 per cent said that they did so several times

Table 6.1   Media usage in Britain, 2008

Time spent in the average weekday	Television (%)	Radio (%)	Newspapers (%)
None	3.3	26.8	30.2
Up to one hour	19.8	32.8	57.0
One to two hours	31.3	13.7	10.4
Two to three hours	25.3	7.4	1.7
More than three hours	20.3	20.3	0.6

Source: European Social Survey, 2008; see http://www.europeansocialsurvey.org/.

a week. Clearly, when individuals have access to the internet they appear to use it extensively.

Much of the usage of the media in Table 6.1 is not political in any meaningful sense of the word. Clearly, some people will positively avoid political coverage on television or in newspapers and confine their attention to soap operas, sports and entertainment programmes or features in magazines. However, the European Social Survey carried an additional set of questions which asked respondents how much time they spent on media consumption of news, politics and current affairs. These questions make it possible to identify the political media users and the responses appear in Table 6.2.

The European Social Survey data in Table 6.2 indicates that, not surprisingly, Britons spent only a proportion of their time on news, politics and current affairs when they were accessing the media. In the case of television 7 per cent of viewers avoided all current affairs and news programmes, but 71 per cent of them spent up to an hour a day viewing these types of programme. Most commonly, this would involve watching a daily news programme, rather than any specialist current affairs programmes or political documentaries. But this is nonetheless a fairly large group of individuals. Again radio listeners were more likely to avoid current affairs programmes than television viewers but some two-thirds of them still spent up to an hour a day on news and current affairs. Finally, it is clear that news dominated the media consumption of newspaper readers, since very few readers appeared to use newspapers exclusively for non-news items such as sports or gossip columns.

Who then are the media users in Britain? Table 6.3 looks at the relationship between the social background characteristics of British respondents in the European Social Survey and their media consumption. A political media-usage scale was constructed, in order to investigate this

Table 6.2   Media usage for news, politics and current affairs in Britain, 2008

Time spent in the average weekday	Television (%)	Radio (%)	Newspapers (%)
None	7.0	17.3	13.2
Up to one hour	71.0	66.5	81.5
One to two hours	17.8	10.3	4.5
Two to three hours	3.0	3.0	0.6
More than three hours	1.3	2.9	0.2

Source: European Social Survey, 2008; see http://www.europeansocialsurvey.org/.

relationship, by combining the indicators in Table 6.2 into a single summary scale. Thus individuals who scored highly on using television, radio and newspaper to obtain political information would also score highly on the summary political media-usage scale. The latter was subsequently divided into three categories which appear in Table 6.3, and which shows the relationship between media usage and the social background characteristics of respondents such as their gender, age and occupational status.

Table 6.3 shows that men were more likely to use the media for political information than women, since almost 21 per cent of them were high users compared with only 15.5 per cent of women. It also shows a relationship between educational attainment and media usage with 20 per cent of highly educated users using the media for political information, compared with only 16 per cent of the less educated users. The relationship between media usage and occupational status, the key indicator of social class, was also quite strong. More than a quarter of high-status senior managers were heavy media users, whereas only 13.6 per cent of low-status unskilled workers fall into this category. Finally, the strongest relationships in the table are between media usage and age. Only 6.8 per cent of the youngest group were heavy media users for politics whereas 27.8 per cent of the oldest group fall into this category. This reflects the fact that people generally pay more attention to politics and current affairs once they pass their mid-twenties and begin to acquire mortgages, family responsibilities and other social ties (Pattie, Seyd and Whiteley, 2004).

Table 6.3 provides a snapshot of media usage in Britain in 2008, but the European Social Survey has carried the same media questions in all of its surveys between 2002 and 2008. This is a relatively short period of time, but it is nonetheless interesting to chart changes in media con-

Table 6.3   Media usage for politics by social background characteristics in Britain

Social characteristics	Low	Medium	High
Gender			
Male	17.3	62.0	20.8
Female	24.6	59.9	15.5
Education			
Up to 10 years' education	30.5	53.3	16.2
10 to 15 years' education	20.0	62.1	17.9
More than 15 years' education	12.7	67.0	20.4
Occupational Status			
Senior manager	11.2	62.5	26.4
Professional occupation	11.8	68.0	20.2
Junior manager and technician	13.3	65.5	21.1
Clerical and administrative worker	17.2	65.0	17.8
Skilled and semi-skilled worker	21.8	60.1	18.1
Unskilled worker	32.2	54.1	13.6
Age			
Up to 26 years of age	33.5	59.6	6.8
26–35	23.2	65.0	11.8
36–45	17.8	66.4	15.7
46–55	16.9	64.3	18.8
56–65	15.6	59.5	24.9
More than 65	20.9	51.3	27.8

Note: The five category measures of media usage of television, radio and newspapers in the surveys are combined into one scale with a range from 1 to 15. Low media usage is defined as scores from 1 to 3, medium media usage scores from 4 to 6, and high usage scores from 7 to 15.

Source: European Social Survey, 2008; see http://www.europeansocialsurvey.org/.

sumption in the four surveys during these years. Table 6.4 shows trends in television, radio and newspaper usage for politics from 2002 to 2008, with only small changes in media usage over this relatively short period of time. It appears that all three media experienced modest increases in usage for political news after 2006. This is apparent in the 'up to an hour' category in the responses which increased for all three media in 2008. This probably occurred when Gordon Brown took over as Prime Minister from Tony Blair in 2007 and a general election appeared imminent at the time. This served to raise interest in politics and so media consumption followed suit.

The really dramatic change, which occurred in media usage over the six years from 2002 to 2008, was on the internet. In 2002, some 56 per cent of respondents reported that they had no access to the internet or

Table 6.4   Changes in media usage for politics in Britain, 2002–8

Time spent in the average weekday	2002 (%)	2004 (%)	2006 (%)	2008 (%)
Television				
None	7.4	8.9	10.6	7.0
Up to an hour	65.3	65.4	66.4	71.0
One to two hours	20.8	18.2	16.7	17.8
Two to three hours	3.9	4.7	4.3	3.0
More than three hours	2.7	2.9	2.0	1.3
Radio				
None	23.6	24.0	26.2	17.3
Up to an hour	57.6	59.3	56.3	66.5
One to two hours	10.8	9.6	10.5	10.3
Two to three hours	4.0	4.3	4.0	3.0
More than three hours	4.1	2.8	3.1	2.9
Newspapers				
None	21.5	27.1	26.2	13.2
Up to an hour	72.1	65.9	56.3	81.5
One to two hours	4.9	5.8	10.5	4.5
Two to three hours	1.0	0.9	4.0	0.6
More than three hours	0.4	0.3	3.1	0.2

Source: European Social Survey, 2002 to 2008; see http://www.europeansocialsurvey.org/.

that they never used it, and only 38 per cent of respondents who used the internet reported using it every day. But as we saw earlier by 2008 this was very different with only 30 per cent reporting no access or no use and 61 per cent stating that they logged on every day. Internet usage, therefore, is rapidly growing in Britain both in relation to access and also usage. Unfortunately, the European Social Survey does not ask about the use of the internet for politics and current affairs, so information on how much that has grown during this period is not available.

However, the 2010 British Election Study survey included many questions about the use of electronic media such as email, Facebook and Twitter by the parties during the election campaign. Party professionals and activists in Britain sought to emulate the highly successful Obama Presidential campaign of 2008 in the United States where electronic media played a key role in raising money and mobilizing voters. However, their efforts did not really pay off on anything like the scale of the Obama campaign. The general conclusion from the survey analysis was that the electronic media played a relatively minor role in the campaign in Britain. This can be gauged from the fact that 43 per cent of respondents in the survey said that they had been contacted by the

Conservatives during the campaign, but only 6 per cent reported being contacted by the party using electronic media. Equivalent figures for Labour and the Liberal Democrats were 40 per cent and 38 per cent reporting contact by these parties, with only 3 per cent reporting electronic contact in both cases. The 2010 general election in Britain was not an internet election. Table 6.3 shows that media usage in Britain has a class, age and educational bias to it with high-status individuals using the media more than lower-status individuals. Having mapped out the profile of media usage in Britain, in the next section we start to examine the effects of the media on public opinion and political behaviour.

Media influences on public opinion

To reiterate an earlier point, a key fact about modern politics is that much of what citizens know about the world is the product of impersonal influences, rather than direct experience. As this discussion indicates, impersonal influence refers to the effects of people's perceptions of the attitudes and beliefs of other people who are anonymous 'others', as opposed to people they know personally. People have to take into account both personal and impersonal sources of information if they are to make sense of the political world.

One example of the distinction between personal and impersonal influence relates to the economy. Citizens can evaluate their own economic circumstances from direct experience and that of their family, but an evaluation of the economic circumstances of the country as a whole has to come from impersonal 'others' via the media. This distinction is a key one in research into media and politics. On the one hand, mediated channels of information cannot be trusted in the same way as direct experience can but on the other hand, such channels provide expertise and knowledge which individuals are unlikely to possess. While an individual can easily pass judgement on the financial situation of their own family, they are unlikely to be able to do so for the country as a whole and therefore they will rely on information from an impersonal source.

This distinction has implications for the influence of the media on voters. The evidence from a series of studies suggests that the media are able to change people's views about trends in mass or collective opinions – about what other people are perceived to think – but they find it much harder to change what the individual themselves think. Mutz illustrates this point with an example:

The media are far more likely to convince people that public attitudes to abortion have become increasingly favourable than they are to alter people's personal attitudes towards the issue. (Mutz 1998: 5)

One illustrative example of this distinction relates to crime. In the 1990s there was considerable controversy surrounding the issue of violent crime in the United States. According to polls the public became convinced that crime had risen in the US in the 1980s and 1990s which is why President Clinton introduced a crime bill at that time. However, the objective crime data did not support this inference – violent crime was no higher in the 1990s than in the 1970s even though many people felt that it was. A similar mismatch in perceptions occurs in Britain. The explanation for this difference is that when people make judgements about crime in general they are responding to impersonal influence from the media which is highly selective in its coverage of crime. When crime declines the media tend to think that this is a temporary phenomenon and so do not give it much coverage. When crime increases they cover it extensively because they see it as the start of a trend.

One of the key characteristic of contemporary society is that impersonal relationships between individuals have proliferated and grown more important over time. A striking example of this relates to the use of credit cards which are now more or less universal, although at one time, in the not too distant past, they did not exist. To make the system of credit card transactions work trust in strangers is required, even though security checks facilitate their use. The Nobel-prize-winning economist Kenneth Arrow underlined this point when he wrote:

Virtually every commercial transaction has within itself an element of trust, certainly any transaction conducted over a period of time. It can be plausibly argued that much of the economic backwardness of the world can be explained by the lack of mutual confidence. (1972: 345)

For credit cards to work the relationship between their users involves the mediation of complex information technologies, dispersed markets and multi-national organizations which are far removed from face-to-face relationships between people. Thus the modern credit economy is only possible because people are willing to trust impersonal 'others'. The growth of impersonal relationships does not of course mean that a decline in direct relationships has occurred, but a gap has opened up between direct and indirect communication with impersonal relationships growing ever more important. These trends explain the gap between perceptions of individuals' personal experiences and their collective judgements about the whole of society. In effect there is a disjunction between the personal and social levels of judgement.

There is now quite a bit of evidence to suggest that personal experience is only weakly connected to political judgements about society in general. To illustrate this point, the gap between the two can be seen in the 2010 British Election Study and relates to citizens' personal experiences of prosperity and their national evaluations of the state of the economy. The study carried two questions which asked about these matters. They were:

1. How does the financial situation of your household now compare with what it was 12 months ago?
2. How do you think the general economic situation in this country has changed over the last 12 months?

These two questions are very similar in wording and they were located close together in the questionnaire, so we should expect them to be strongly related if personal experience is the key driver of national judgements of the economy. The relationship between the responses to the two questions can be observed in Table 6.5. Reading the table by rows, it shows that 73 per cent of respondents who thought that their own personal finances had become much worse in the previous year, also thought that the national economy had become much worse over the same period of time. On the face of it this suggests a close relationship between the two, but further down the table no less than 31 per cent of people who felt that their own personal finances had grown better also thought that the national economy had grown worse – polar opposite answers. So while there is clearly an association between the two measures, the association is not that strong.

To clarify this, the weakness of the relationship can be seen in the table where the figures on the main diagonal from the top left to the bottom right are highlighted. These are individuals who give the same answer to both questions, and only 31 per cent of all respondents are in these categories. In other words nearly 70 per cent answered the first question differently from the second question. To reinforce this point, no-one at all thought that their personal finances and the national economy had both become much better. This indicates quite a disjunction between personal experience and mediated experience. So it is hard

Table 6.5   The relationship between personal and national economic evaluations, 2010

Personal finances (row percentages)	National economic evaluations				
	A lot worse	A little worse	The same	A little better	A lot better
A lot worse	**73.0**	15.2	5.9	5.3	0.6
A little worse	53.0	**28.9**	9.2	8.3	0.6
The same	27.9	40.9	**15.0**	15.8	0.5
A little better	21.9	32.8	14.4	**30.3**	0.5
A lot better	31.3	16.7	14.6	37.5	**0.0**

Source: British Election Study Face-to-Face Pre-Election Survey (BES, 2010).

to conclude from this table that personal experience of the economy is the sole driver of perceptions of the national economy.

To return to an earlier point, the media do not influence personal experience very much, but they can influence collective experience, or perceptions that the state of the national economy is getting better or worse. Personal experience tends to influence personal judgements rather than societal or collective judgements. With these points in mind, in the next section we explore ways in which the media can influence collective judgements, before considering what this might mean for voting behaviour.

The role of the mass media in influencing collective perceptions

The media can influence collective judgements in a variety of ways. Research has shown that influence works through five different mechanisms: agenda setting, priming, risk perceptions, cultivation and learning. We explain these in more detail below.

Agenda setting refers to the function of the media in influencing what people think about, rather than what they actually think. At any one point of time, the political agenda is a moving target which shifts in the light of events, political conflicts, debates and policy decisions made by government. The media tends both to follow and to create this agenda and by focusing on a limited set of issues and ignoring others, the media exercises influence. The existence of such an agenda is an inevitable consequence of the complexity of modern politics. If the media and their users are not to be swamped then they have to focus, but this means that some important issues get ignored while other issues are brought into prominence. This agenda can be rather artificial however. Sanders and Gavin (2004) found that voter perceptions of the state of the national economy were driven by the news agenda to a much greater extent than they were by the objective state of the economy as measured by unemployment and inflation. Perceptions of economic performance were following a media agenda, which was not the same as the reality.

A second mechanism is priming, which refers to the way in which agenda setting works. When the media pay attention to some problems and ignore others they are altering the standards which people use to evaluate the performance of the government or political leaders in handling these problems. By making some issues more accessible in people's minds, media priorities prime individuals to attach more weight to certain issues than to others – news stories manipulate the 'accessibility' of issues in people's minds rather than perceptions of whether or not a problem is getting better or worse. Clearly, this process can favour some political leaders or parties over others, if the issues that are prominent are the ones on which they perform well, and their failures are kept in the background. The role of priming was explored in particular by Iyengar (1991) in his research on the influence of television coverage of politics on public opinion. By highlighting some issues and ignoring others, political debates will become skewed in a certain direction.

One important finding in this research is that the media can alter people's perceptions of the risks associated with everyday life, such as the effects of diseases, accidents or crime. This is the basis of the 'media malaise' hypothesis or the idea that the media accentuates the negative and plays down the positive in the way that it reports politics. Research shows that people are more responsive to negative information about politics from the media than to positive information (Ronis and Lipinski, 1985; Soroka, 2006), explaining why the media concentrate on scandals, disasters and threats to the everyday lives of citizens. This bias can make people more fearful about crime, for example, than is objectively justified by the actual risks of crime. Repeated exposure to stories about crime will eventually change people's perceptions of their chances of being the victims of crime. However, to repeat an earlier point, it appears that the media primarily affects people's evaluation of collective risks of crime, rather than the personal risk. Thus news about crime makes people think that it is a growing social problem, but they are slower to conclude that they will personally be a victim of crime.

The cultivation hypothesis argues that television in particular has the capacity to cultivate misperceptions of reality in its viewers. The earliest work on this issue, Gerbner *et al.* (1980), suggested that television drama cultivates a distorted perception of reality in relation to violent crime. Ansolabehere and Iyengar (1995) showed that watching negative campaigns on television had the effect of reducing the citizen's willingness to vote. In effect it made individuals feel that no politician could be trusted and therefore they should opt out of the political process altogether. Capella and Jamieson (1997) suggested that there may be a 'spiral of cynicism' among the public caused by watching news coverage of politics and campaigns as a result of largely negative coverage of political actors and the political process.

In contrast Mutz (1998) argues that there is little support for the argument that television leads to greater personal fear or mistrust of others. In her view, the impacts are impersonal in nature, relating to the probability of crime in society rather than personal fear of crime. In general, people do not consider television to depict reality, preventing the cultivation hypothesis from being a significant factor in citizen perceptions of politics. However, it should be said that there is evidence to suggest that negative campaigning can reduce citizen trust in government (Fridkin and Kenney, 2004). This implies that if the political discourse is very negative, this is likely to undermine civic engagement.

The cultivation hypothesis is really about how people learn from the media. When the media content accurately reflects social and political realities, people's acceptance of this involves political learning. The media is often negative and sensational, but if the media malaise hypothesis is correct then we would expect to see heavy media users being less interested in politics, more cynical about politicians, and having a lower sense of efficacy than infrequent media users. We can examine the relationship between media usage and indicators of interest in politics, trust in politicians and efficacy, in the European Social Survey data, and find there is little support for the 'media malaise' hypothesis. In fact, high media users are the most interested in politics, the most likely to trust politicians and are the least likely to think that politics is so complicated that they can't understand it. For example, 24 per cent of low media users are very or fairly interested in politics, compared with 30 per cent of high media users. Similarly, 49 per cent of low media users regularly think that politics is too complicated for them to understand compared with only 26 per cent of high media users.

Clearly, media usage appears to promote political interest, political trust and political efficacy rather than the opposite. This is consistent with the findings in Chapter 3 in which the cognitive engagement model was discussed as one of the important theoretical explanations of political participation. This model is all about contact and engagement with the media and it suggests that high media users participate more than their low media user counterparts. These positive relationships suggest that while media malaise may exist, it does not appear to counteract the more beneficial effects of media exposure such as knowing more about politics and having a better understanding of the political process.

Methodological issues

There is a key methodological problem associated with attempts to identify media effects in politics. The problem is that it is difficult to isolate the causal processes at work. If, for example, someone regularly reads a newspaper, which is aligned with the political party they support, this could be because they chose the party to fit the newspaper or alternatively it could be that they chose the newspaper to fit the party. The first alternative implies that the media can have an important influence on politics, whereas the second implies weak or non-existent media effects. Norris *et al.* (1999) addressed this problem with the assistance of a panel survey in which respondents were interviewed on more than one occasion. This helps to untangle causal relationships because one can take advantage of sequences of responses over time to explore relationships. Since attitudes and behaviour measured in the future cannot influence those measured in the past that makes it easier to identify causal processes. Their research suggests that newspapers tend to have a limited influence on their readers with respect to voting behaviour, and the strongest effects came from mobilizing already committed voters to actually turn out on the day.

Zaller (1996) challenges this view by suggesting that media effects are in fact massive but this can be seen only if they are measured properly. In this view, much of the existing work on media effects finds non-existent or weak effects because they are not using the correct measures. To this end he introduces the concept of the *reception gap*. This is the gap between the perceptions of different news stories associated with different types of citizen. He illustrates this idea with data on the diffusion of two news stories throughout the US population. One was the crash of a DC-10 airliner, a dramatic incident which took place in 1989, and which received a great deal of coverage. He argued that the typical 'busy citizen' who pays a modest attention to the news would have a high chance of knowing about this event.

Zaller's second much less prominent story was the resignation of Jim Wright, the speaker of the House of Representatives in 1989, following accusations of corruption. Zaller argued that the 'busy citizen' would only have a modest chance of knowing about this event because the coverage of it was much less widespread. The difference between the impacts of these two stories is the reception gap. If the two stories were competing persuasive messages during an election campaign, for example, then we would expect to see a much larger number of people being influenced by the first message than the second. Zaller's point is that if this reception gap is taken into account when media effects are measured then they are much bigger than many existing studies have suggested.

We can examine this important question in Britain with a case study, the impact of the *Sun* newspaper on voting behaviour when it changed its support from the Conservatives to Labour between the 1992 and 1997 elections. This change was a major event in the run up to the Labour victory of 1997 since the *Sun* had the largest circulation of any newspaper in Britain. So the question is, did this change of allegiance by the newspaper influence the behaviour of voters?

A case study – the *Sun* backs New Labour

The *Sun* newspaper produced a memorable headline after John Major's victory in the general election of 1992: 'It's the Sun Wot Won It'. In other words ,the editors claimed that their strong support for the Conservatives had swung the election for John Major. But did the newspaper really win the election in 1992? And more generally, can newspapers influence the voting behaviour of their readers? Once again, a key problem in testing this idea is that of causality. Did *Sun* readers tend to support the Conservatives because of their paper's editorial line, or was it because they were Tories to begin with and for that reason chose to read the *Sun*?

If we compare the 1992 and 1997 general elections in Britain, they provide something of a natural experiment which can test the relationship between voting and newspaper readership. In 1992 the *Sun* was implacably opposed to Labour and relentlessly attacked Neil Kinnock, the Labour leader at that time. By 1997 the paper gave Tony Blair a relatively lukewarm endorsement rather late on in the campaign, but it was nonetheless a significant change of its editorial line. The relentless attacks on Labour declined and the paper was much more critical of the Conservatives than it had been in 1992. Since the *Sun*'s endorsement of Labour came only rather late in the run-up to the election in 1997 it is unlikely that this prompted many people to start buying the newspaper because they were already Labour voters. It is much more likely that any differences between the voting patterns of *Sun* readers in 1992 and 1997 were explained, at least in part, by the change in the paper's allegiance.

Given that the outcomes of the 1992 and 1997 elections were very different, it is important to take into account the fact that even if the *Sun* had no effect at all on its reader's political preferences we would still observe differences between *Sun* readers in 1992 and 1997. This is because other factors were at work in influencing their voting behaviour apart from the editorial line of the newspaper. One way to get round this problem is to compare *Sun* readers with *Daily Mirror* readers, in what amounts to a type of experiment. Both the *Sun* and the *Daily Mirror* are tabloid newspapers with large working-class readerships that tend to be less educated and are generally employed in blue-collar occupations. Thus the social background characteristics of the readers of the two newspapers are rather similar and quite different from those of broadsheet newspapers such as the *Guardian* and *Daily Telegraph*.

If newspapers have a great deal of influence over their readers, then differences in voting patterns between *Sun* readers and *Daily Mirror* readers should have narrowed in 1997 compared with 1992, since the *Mirror* remained loyal to Labour throughout. In other words the *Sun*'s endorsement of New Labour should have made their readers behave rather more like *Mirror* readers. Other factors are at work in explaining voting behaviour apart from editorial endorsements, however, the readerships of the two newspapers are very similar in their social characteristics and these other factors should act in a rather similar way for both types of readers. For example, if social class played a more prominent role in explaining voting behaviour in one election compared with the other, this would work in the same way for both the *Sun* and the *Daily Mirror* readers, because their social class characteristics are rather similar. The really big difference between the two newspapers was the change in the *Sun*'s endorsement of Labour in 1997 compared with 1992. So the two elections and two newspapers provide a natural experiment for examining this question.

The idea can be examined with data from the British Election Studies of 1992 and 1997, both consisting of large-scale surveys of the electorate undertaken immediately after polling day. Both surveys included questions about newspaper readership and so it is possible to identify the voting patterns of *Sun* and *Daily Mirror* readers in both elections. Table 6.6 includes the data from this analysis and it can be seen that in 1992 there were large differences between the voting of *Sun* and *Daily*

Table 6.6   The relationship between voting behaviour and newspaper readership, 1992–7

	1992 vote	*1997 vote*	*Change*
Sun readers			
Conservative	39	23	−16
Labour	30	38	+8
Liberal Democrat	12	9	−3
Did not vote	20	31	−11
Daily Mirror readers			
Conservative	14	6	−8
Labour	63	71	+8
Liberal Democrat	10	8	−2
Did not vote	12	16	+4

Source: British Election Studies, 1992 and 1997.

Mirror readers, even though their social characteristics were rather similar.

The table also shows that by 1997 political differences between the readerships of the two papers narrowed in relation to Conservative voting, but not for Labour voting. Thus support for the Conservatives among *Sun* readers fell by 16 per cent between the two elections (from 39 per cent to 23 per cent) but by only 8 per cent (from 14 per cent to 6 per cent) for *Daily Mirror* readers. On the other hand, support for Labour increased by 8 per cent for the readers of both papers, although it started from a much higher base in the case of the *Mirror*. One very noticeable change between the two elections involved the readers who did not vote. About a fifth of *Sun* readers failed to turn out in 1992, but this increased massively to nearly a third by 1997. In contrast, the increase in non-voting among *Mirror* readers was a modest 4 per cent. So it appears that the *Sun*'s switch from strong support for the Tories to lukewarm support for New Labour had the effect of discouraging *Sun* readers either from voting Conservative or from voting at all. It did not appear to have the effect of encouraging them to vote Labour, or for that matter Liberal Democrat. This illustrates the point that newspapers are better at mobilizing their readers to vote, or in this case to stay home, than they are at changing their readers' voting habits.

Clearly, these results do not precisely explain the mechanisms by which newspaper editorials influence their readers. The results are probably the product of agenda setting, priming and some of the other mechanisms discussed earlier. But it appears that newspapers can influence the voters, although this may vary depending on the political context. Long-standing Conservatives who were fed up with the Tory government in 1997, appear to have been tipped over the edge to vote down John Major's government, or to abstain from voting altogether by the *Sun*'s change of editorial direction.

But what difference does this make to elections, since in 1997 Labour won by a landslide? The answer is that it might be quite important, and a thought experiment illustrates why. Imagine that the *Sun* had not endorsed New Labour in 1997, and this had the effect of producing changes in Conservative voting and in abstention among their readers very similar to those which occurred among *Daily Mirror* readers. This would mean that Conservative voting among *Sun* readers would have declined by 8 per cent instead of 16 per cent, and that abstention would have increased by 4 per cent instead of 11 per cent. A quick calculation shows that this scenario would have given the Conservatives an extra half a million votes, assuming that the bulk of the non-voters were Tories. Depending on where they lived these voters would have significantly changed the party composition of the House of Commons. This would not have changed the outcome of the election in 1997, but it could have made a difference to the result of a closer election.

In the 2010 general election no party attained an overall majority, and once again the *Sun* returned to supporting the Conservatives, so it is possible that Labour might have won a few more seats if it had retained the endorsement of the *Sun*. In fact the readership of the *Sun* has fallen significantly along with that of most other newspapers since the 1990s, so if these effects are still at work they are likely to be weaker than in the past. Once again the newspaper may not have changed the outcome of the election, but it might have made a Liberal Democrat–Labour coalition government a possibility.

Conclusion

The discussion of media effects and impersonal influences in this chapter shows that the media can influence political attitudes and voting behaviour in Britain. There are various mechanisms through which this influence is exercised, such as, agenda setting, priming and the other processes discussed earlier. Thus, the media are important players in influencing the state of citizenship in Britain and, potentially, can influence all aspects of citizenship including norms, values, voluntary activity and participation and, most importantly, voting behaviour.

Understanding the media is relevant for understanding how citizenship is created and maintained in the long run.

Television, radio and newspapers are all going through a period of rapid change in Britain. As far as the electronic media are concerned, the era of broadcasting, in which programmes are targeted at the whole population who watch the same television channels or listen to the same radio programmes, is giving way to an era of narrowcasting. In the world of narrowcasting, programmes are targeted at specific niche groups and individuals seek out the programmes they want rather than just accepting what is provided. The origins of this lie in the proliferation of television and radio channels via cable and satellite and the growth of the internet which has meant that media markets have fragmented and audiences are smaller.

This process has been accelerated by the rapid growth in the internet described earlier, since the internet is a narrowcasting rather than a broadcasting medium. The internet adds the dimension of interaction between the broadcaster and audience. In addition, blogging and social networking means that individuals can, in effect, become broadcasters themselves. The proliferation of choices in media markets brings with it advantages to consumers who can find the programmes they like and ignore the rest. But it creates problems for the political process and for social cohesion. There is a risk that in a world where individuals narrowcast they choose media outlets they agree with and ignore the ones that they do not. This has the effect of reinforcing attitudes and cementing prejudices, since citizens face no challenges to their beliefs posed by alternative viewpoints. Narrowcasting has the potential of polarizing debates and political attitudes, since it undermines dialogue between groups with different opinions. To reiterate a point made in Chapter 5, it is similar to the distinction between bonding and bridging in the social capital literature: bonding produces tight-knit media communities which talk to each other but not to everyone else, whereas bridging brings media communities together.

A second challenge to the media in Britain is the decline in newspaper circulation over time, referred to earlier. Writing in the *Press Gazette* in September 2010, Oliver Luft pointed out that:

The average daily circulation of *The Times* newspaper dropped below half-a-million in August as all national newspapers suffered a year-on-year decline in sales. The News International daily was one of six national papers to suffer a double-digit year-on-year fall in circulation last month as it hit a 16-year circulation low.

Newspapers have been struggling to deal with the growth of the internet and the challenge of acquiring new revenue streams when the public have been socialized into expecting internet content to be free. The practice of giving away the content of print newspapers on the internet is ultimately commercially unsustainable, but there are few signs that newspapers as a whole have solved that particular conundrum at the present time. News International has placed the content of its newspapers such as *The Times* behind paywalls but it is unclear at the time of writing if this experiment has been successful.

From the point of view of civic culture, the decline of the print media would be no great problem if the rise of the electronic media fulfilled the same function of providing in-depth coverage of politics and government. But it is not at all clear that the internet does this. The rise of the blogosphere has created new forms of political participation, but the content of blogs can be wildly inaccurate, although this may not matter greatly if they get people involved. The average citizen has less reason to trust the internet for political information than traditional outlets such as television and radio, where statutory standards relating to balance and coverage apply. More generally, the internet has made the retrieval of facts very much easier than in the past, with information being easily accessible by Google and Wikipedia. The problem for the citizen is one of making sense of all this information and being able to trust the sources. This is a real problem for the 'busy citizen'.

Up to this point we have examined norms, attitudes and actions which underpin the civic culture in Britain. But to get a clearer picture of the state of citizenship we need to make comparisons with other countries. Are we above average or below average in our rates of participation and volunteering? Are our norms and values similar to, or different from, those in other countries? To address these questions we focus on comparative evidence in the next chapter.

7

Britain in Comparative Perspective

Following the financial crisis of 2007–9 and the subsequent recession, governments across the democratic world faced the task of cutting back on public expenditure in order to deal with ballooning deficits. The size and scope of cuts are, of course, highly controversial and even though they have been forced on governments by events they do raise fundamental questions. Perhaps the most important question is: are governments trying to do too much? There is the argument that the state has become too large and it is time for it to withdraw from some activities and let the private sector take over. The Conservative–Liberal Democrat coalition government which formed in Britain after the 2010 general election brought the issue of cuts in public expenditure into the forefront of debate. The coalition plans large-scale cuts in public services in order to deal with the deficit.

In this chapter we look at the scope of government in Britain in comparison with other advanced industrial countries and address the question of why government has become so large and if anything should be done about it. This can only be effectively studied using a comparative approach, which looks at the UK experience in relation to other industrialized countries. In the absence of such an approach, it is hard to identify factors which are unique to one country and those which are common to many. Therefore, this chapter examines the determinants of the size of governments across the industrial world.

We begin by looking at Britain's position in relation to other OECD (Organisation for Economic Co-operation and Development) countries, that is, the world's most advanced industrial democracies. The aim is to see if Britain is an outlier in any sense, both objectively, in terms of actual government spending and subjectively, in terms of what people think about the scope of government. This is followed by a discussion of why government is so large and whether it can or should be reduced in size in the future.

Is government too big?

The starting point for addressing the size of the state is to look at government spending as a percentage of Gross Domestic Product (GDP) in the advanced countries. In this way it is possible to see where Britain is located in comparison with other rather similar countries. Figure 7.1 shows government spending in twenty-eight OECD countries, including Britain, during the period 1995–2000 (Easterly, 2001; Teorell *et al.*, 2010). At one end of the scale are the relatively low-spending countries, such as Mexico, the United States and Switzerland and at the other end there are countries, such as Belgium, France and the Netherlands, all of which are high spenders. As the figure shows Britain was in the fourteenth or median position with just over 36 per cent of GDP spent by the government. In other words Britain is average in this respect.

Another approach to the same issue is to examine the total tax take of governments, again with the idea of determining how Britain features in relation to other OECD countries. This is shown in Figure 7.2 which examines all taxes and social security payments as a percentage of GDP in the same twenty-eight OECD countries. The ranking of countries is rather similar to that of Figure 7.1, except in this case Britain was just above the median in the twentieth position with a tax take of just under 35 per cent of GDP. The high tax-paying countries were largely the same

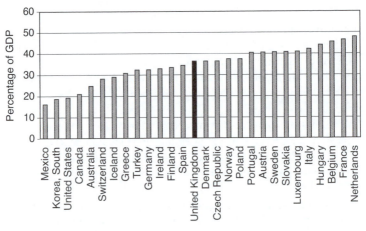

Source: Teorell *et al.*, 2010.

Figure 7.1   Government expenditure as a percentage of GDP 2000 OECD countries, 1995–2000

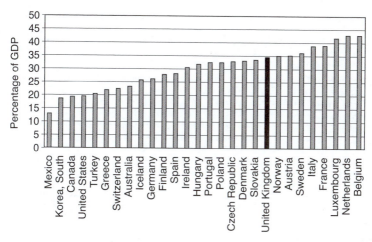

Source: Teorell *et al.*, 2010.

Figure 7.2   Taxes and social security payments as a percentage of GDP in 28 OECD countries, 1995–2000

as the high-spending countries such as Belgium, the Netherlands and France. Taken together these two figures suggest that Britain is in the mainstream of countries with respect to public expenditure and taxation and therefore has an average sized government.

It is also the case that government spending has grown rather dramatically in the long run in these countries. One analysis demonstrated that government expenditure averaged 10.8 per cent of GDP in fourteen industrial countries in 1870, but averaged 45 per cent of GDP by 1996 in these same countries (Tanzi and Schuknecht, 2000). Figure 7.3 shows trends in public expenditure as a percentage of Gross Domestic Product in the OECD countries over the period of a generation from 1972 to 1999. During these years, spending increased considerably from about a quarter of national income or GDP, to more than a third. So there is clearly an important political trend at work in these countries. So why has this growth occurred and how does Britain look in relation to this trend? We address this next.

The growth of government in comparative perspective

Not surprisingly, there is a great deal of literature that seeks to explain trends in the growth of government over time (Peacock and Wiseman,

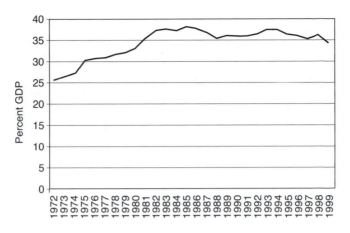

Source: Quality of Government Time Series; see http://www.qog.pol.gu.se.

Figure 7.3   The growth in government spending as a percentage of GDP in OECD countries, 1972–99

1961; Niskanen, 1971; Buchanan and Wagner, 1977; Borcherding, 1977; Peltzman, 1980; Brennan and Buchanan, 1980; Kau and Rubin, 1981; Meltzer and Richard, 1981; Holcombe, 1994, 2005; Persson and Tabellini, 1999). Holcombe (2005) classifies explanations of government growth into three types; first, those which stress the role of rent-seeking or budget maximizing behaviour by bureaucrats and organizations in bringing this about. These are 'supply side' explanations of government growth, since they stress factors which influence the supply of government. Second, there are explanations which emphasize the role of ordinary citizens in demanding more government services and regulation, or 'demand side' explanations.

A third group of theories, which are combinations of demand and supply side explanations, stress the importance of path dependencies in the growth of government. In this case 'ratchet' effects occur when wars or financial crises produce big increases in government spending and policy outputs, which do not subsequently return to pre-crisis levels (Peacock and Wiseman, 1961). These ratchet effects can be explained both by bureaucratic inertia and also by an increased demand for government on the part of the public, that is, a combination of demand and supply factors.

To begin with supply-side explanations first, the starting point of this approach was a book by Niskanen (1971) *Bureaucracy and Representative Government*. He argued that government bureaucrats pursue their own personal objectives rather than more general social goals and so they try to maximize their budgets in a way that is directly analogous to profit maximizing by private-sector entrepreneurs. They can achieve higher salaries and perquisites for themselves if they have more staff and bigger budgets, therefore, the motivating force of this supply-side explanation is rent-seeking by bureaucrats. A situation that is caused by a principal-agent problem in the relationship between political oversight agencies, typically legislatures, and policy-implementing bureaucracies.

Oversight agencies (the principles) are unable to identify the true costs of policies without the help of the bureaucracies (the agents) whom they are overseeing and thus allows the bureaucrats to extract rents or profits by exaggerating the costs of government services. The result is an over-supply of government compared with a situation where principals have an accurate knowledge of costs. In this view bureaucracies have a tendency to seek out new opportunities for acquiring responsibilities, taking on more staff and spending additional money and this is at the root of the growth of government. Niskanen's work stimulated a number of studies that developed this idea (Borcherding, 1977; Romer and Rosenthal, 1979; Brennan and Buchanan, 1980; Kau and Rubin, 1981).

A further supply-side explanation is based on rent-seeking by interest groups rather than by bureaucrats (Olson, 1965, 1982; Stigler, 1971; Pelzman, 1980; Mueller and Murrell, 1986; Rice 1986). In this case, special interest groups seek benefits for themselves by persuading legislatures to fund programmes or to impose regulations, both of which lead to a growth in government. An example of this is the Common Agricultural Policy which subsidizes European farmers at the expense of their competitors in the developing world and also at the expense of European consumers. This occurs as the concentration of benefits on the special interest group members make the per capita returns to lobbying high, thereby providing a strong incentive for them to seek such benefits. In contrast, the average cost per citizen of special interest lobbying is rather small because it is spread widely throughout society, thus reducing the incentives of voters to oppose rent-seeking. This asymmetry produces a growth in government since advocates of spending are more politically active and influential than their opponents. European farmers were assiduous in lobbying for these subsidies in the early years of the European Community in the 1950s and have fought to protect them ever since.

These supply-side explanations of government growth do face problems, however. First, a large component of the growth of government has been a rise of transfer payments between individual citizens such as pensions, unemployment benefits and social security. It is not at all clear how these can be explained by rent-seeking bureaucrats. The bureaucrats do not directly benefit from such transfer payments, although it might be argued that they indirectly benefit because of the need to administer welfare programmes. However, the evidence to support this idea is weak, since in 2005 there was no association at all between spending on the administrative costs of government, principally public-sector salaries, and spending on social protection in the OECD countries (OECD, 2009). This fact suggests that bureaucrats do not really benefit much by expanding transfer payments.

A similar point can be made about rent-seeking interest groups. The literature on such groups has concentrated almost exclusively on producer interests such as the farm lobby, banks and trade unions (see Olson, 1965). Such organizations represent producers of goods and services and they take an active interest in lobbying government. In contrast, interest groups that represent the poor, the elderly or the unemployed, are all consumer groups and, as such, they represent individuals who are the consumers of benefits rather than producers. In general, such groups lack the political leverage and the resources of producer groups (Whiteley and Winyard, 1986). It is unlikely, therefore, that the rapid increase in transfer payments across the democratic world can be explained by the activities of such groups. Something else must be happening to explain these trends.

A second difficulty with purely supply-side explanations of government growth is that they are inconsistent with demand-side explanations. In particular, pressure from voters should inhibit wasteful bureaucratic rent-seeking. The voters have no interest in supporting bloated bureaucracies although the informational and incentive asymmetries already referred to will allow them to develop. But the rate of growth in government is well above any levels which can be explained by inattentive voters and opportunistic bureaucrats. Apart from anything else politicians seeking re-election have no interest is permitting such rent-seeking if it wastes money, which could otherwise be spent on their constituents and thereby boost their own support.

Turning next to demand-side explanations, these are more diverse than their supply-side counterparts. Unlike supply side explanations, demand-side explanations are based on the idea that voters want more spending. As Figures 7.1 and 7.2 show that there is a strong relationship between taxation and spending, so theories must explain why the voters want more spending and, at the same time, why they are willing to pay more taxes.

Mueller (2003) develops a model which focuses on the demand for spending by the median voter. The median voter is important in his analysis because she is at the centre of the left–right ideological divide in society, and it has long been argued that voters in the centre ground of politics are decisive in determining the outcome of elections (Black, 1958; Downs, 1957). Since parties must win the centre ground of politics where most voters are concentrated if they are to win elections, the median voter takes on great importance.

In Mueller's analysis, this voter's demand for public spending depends on her income and a set of 'taste' variables. An example of a taste variable is the demand for protection from international economic competition which many voters seek (see Rodrik, 1998). Another example is the popularity of government services that gives rise to the well-known 'Baumol effect' (Baumol, 1967). This refers to the fact that public services tend to be inelastic in demand, so that price rises have little effect on the demand for them. Generally, the growth of productivity in public services is slower than the growth of productivity in private-sector manufacturing industries. As a result, public services grow more expensive over time relative to other goods in the economy and this, together with the inelastic demand for government services, has the effect of increasing public spending relative to private sector spending.

As the earlier discussion indicated, the demand for transfer payments is an important reason for the growth of government. The models in the economics literature, which focus on the demand for such payments, concern the redistribution of income between individuals (Meltzer and Richard, 1978, 1981, 1983; Pelzman, 1980). These models assume that individuals on below-average incomes want more spending, and those on above-average incomes want less. The rationale for this is that the former will benefit more than they will pay in taxes, whilst the latter will have the opposite experience. Again, the median voter plays a key role in these models, since they have to explain why she wants more and more public services over time. One such explanation is the change in the characteristics of the median voter caused by the extension of the franchise over time. This has the effect of reducing the income of the median voter because less affluent individuals are joining the electorate. If the median voter is more likely to demand benefits from government than her more affluent predecessors, this will increase spending.

These models do face a key problem though. The timing of the extension of the franchise does not coincide with the big expansion in transfer payments. The franchise had been extended to adults in almost all advanced industrial democracies well before the Second World War and yet the bulk of the expansion of transfer payments occurred after 1945. In Britain, for example, near-universal suffrage was achieved in 1928 when the bulk of women received the vote, but the great increase in government spending took place during the Labour government of 1945–51 and in the post-war years with the rise of the welfare state. Thus these enormous unexplained lags in the process mean that changes in the franchise cannot easily explain the rising demand for government. This is one of the reasons why empirical tests of the Meltzer and Richard model which utilizes this explanation shows little support for their argument (Kristov, Lindert and McClelland, 1992; Gouveia and Masia, 1998).

One of the weaknesses of the demand-side literature is that surprisingly enough the preferences of actual voters are commonly missing from the analysis. Assumptions are made that low-income voters want redistribution and high-income voters want the opposite, but tests of this assumption are rare. One exception to this is Iversen's work on the relationship between labour force participation and the demand for social spending (Iversen, 2005; Iversen and Soskice, 2006). He argues that the Meltzer and Richard model is incomplete since it does not take into account the demand by citizens for insurance against job loss. Such a demand can be significant even among high-status, high-income individuals. This is because employees with very specific job skills are unlikely to get another job with a comparable income if they are laid off, and so they value state-provided social insurance. It is their lack of marketable skills that provides their support for government transfer payments. Iversen's (2005) empirical analysis of individual voter preferences supports this conclusion. The value of this work is that it highlights the importance of risk in explaining the growth of government. Government spending helps individuals to offset various risks and this is true for the affluent as well as the poor.

More generally, the assumption that high-income workers will automatically oppose transfer payments is problematic, since the evidence suggests that the recipients of transfer payments can be found at all levels of the income distribution. It has been shown that middle-income groups receive a large proportion of transfer payments in advanced industrial societies (Atkinson, Rainwater and Smeeding, 1995). Clearly, if transfer payments have only a limited redistributive impact, then income may not be as important as these models assume. The relationship between income and attitudes to transfer payments needs testing rather than assuming.

Following his extensive review of the literature on demand-side explanations of the growth of government Mueller concluded that: 'the hypotheses put forward so far, which attempt to explain the growth of government in simple re-distributional terms, are inadequate' (2003: 519). In the next section we develop a model of the demand for government which attempts to remedy some of these deficiencies.

Theorizing the demand for government

The logic of democracy is that a majority of the people get most of what they want from the political process most of the time. So there is a simple explanation for the growth in government namely that a majority of the voters want it. To understand this we need to focus on the preferences of actual voters and observe how these can influence government policies and public spending over time. Thus the starting point of the present analysis is the proposition that individuals will support public spending if they perceive that the benefits of such spending, both for themselves and the wider society, exceeds the costs in terms of the burden of taxation. However, costs and benefits cannot be understood in terms of a narrowly defined model of individual self-interest which is a near universal assumption in this literature. Instead they should be evaluated in terms that actual voters perceive them (Winter and Mouritzen, 2001).

There is a mass of evidence to suggest that voters evaluate government policy making in 'sociotropic' terms, that is, in relation to the effectiveness of policies in delivering benefits for the whole of society, not just for themselves (Kinder and Kiewiet, 1981). These types of evaluations do not mean that 'egocentric' evaluations, that is, self-interested motives are unimportant. In fact, the literature on voting behaviour suggests that both types of evaluation are influential in explaining party choice and turnout. But a narrowly focused egocentric explanation of the demand for government is likely to miss a large part of the story. Voters are influenced by altruistic concerns and also by the norms and values of the societies in which they live, and these need to be taken into account in understanding the demand for government (Pattie, Seyd and Whiteley, 2004).

Accordingly, the present model explains the demand for government spending in terms of two classes of variables. First, there are their measures of the citizen's egocentric interests in demanding spending, which are determined by their income, their position in the job market, their gender, age and other demographic factors. The argument here is that their interests reflect their position in the social structure, and that position influences their demand for public spending. Poor people are likely to want more spending since it will benefit them and they are unlikely to have to bear the burden in taxation. Similarly, the wealthy will oppose more spending for the same reason; they will end up paying but will not get much of the benefits. This is the type of explanation that has dominated the literature up to this point.

However, the demand for public spending is also influenced by citizen attitudes and values, and these are primarily driven by sociotropic factors. These attitudes relate to views about the proper scope of government, the performance of the state in delivering policies, and the role of government in intervening in the economy and in the market place, the kind of measures we examined in Chapter 2. Such factors have been neglected in the existing literature, but they are crucial to understanding the demand for public spending.

We can get some idea of the importance of these different factors by again using data from the 2006 Role of Government Survey introduced in Chapter 2 (ISSP, 2006). Table 7.1 replicates Table 2.2 in that chapter, which relates to the preferences for public spending, but in this case the data includes respondents from all thirty-two countries in the survey, not just Britain. It may be recalled from the earlier chapter that the highest priorities for spending in Britain were in health, pensions and education. A similar pattern emerges in Table 7.1 with these three taking the pole position in spending priorities. However, it is also apparent that the rest of the democratic world attaches an even higher priority to such spending than do Britons. For example, 27 per cent of Britons thought that the state should spend much more on health, whereas 39 per cent thought this in the other 31 countries. Similar patterns exist for pensions and education. There are also similarities in the two tables with respect to spending on defence and the police, both of which are lower priorities in Britain as well as in the rest of the democratic world. One clear difference relates to spending unemployment benefits, which was a significantly higher priority across the democratic world than it was in Britain.

We can get a better sense of how Britain compares with these countries in general by combining the responses in Table 7.1 into a single 'preferences for spending' scale. This is done simply by adding together the responses for all eight items. If 'spend much less' scores 1; 'spend less' scores 2; 'spend the same' scores 3; 'spend more' scores 4 and 'spend much more' scores 5 for each of the eight spending areas, then

Table 7.1   Preferences for public spending in 32 democracies, 2006

	Spend much less (%)	Spend less (%)	Spend the same (%)	Spend more (%)	Spend much more (%)
Health	0.5	2	14	45	39
Old age pensions	1	3	25	42	30
Education	0.5	2	19	42	36
The police and law enforcement	2	7	34	40	18
The environment	2	6	35	41	17
Defence	10	22	40	20	9
Unemployment benefits	5	15	39	27	14
Culture and the arts	8	16	42	25	9

Source: ISSP, *Role of Government Survey*, 2006 (N=46,669).

adding together these responses produces a scale which varies from 8 (a score of one on each spending area) to 40 (a score of 5 on each spending area). The resulting scale appears in Figure 7.4 where the spending preferences of Britons are included alongside those of the other countries. If an individual wanted to keep spending levels the same for all policy areas they would have a score of 24 on the scale (i.e. 3, the score for the 'same' category, times 8 items).

As Figure 7.4 shows, however, the vast majority of people are above this score, and so want more spending rather than less. The comparison of Britain with the rest of the world is interesting since Britons appear to be less enthusiastic about public spending than their counterparts elsewhere, something which is apparent in Table 7.1. The average score on the scale for Britons was 26.8 compared with 28.0 for all other respondents. These differences are not large, but they do indicate that Britain is not at the high end of the demand for spending scale by international standards.

What of the relationship between the desire for spending and income, the key indicator of egocentric interests? This can be shown by looking at the relationship between the spending scale and income. This is shown in Figure 7.5 where incomes are grouped into five categories. The income data in the Scope of Government data file is measured in

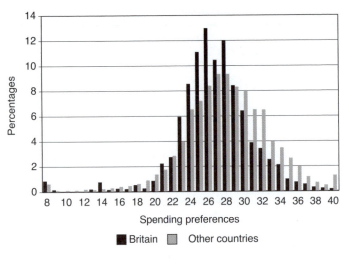

Source: ISSP, *Role of Government Survey, 2006.*

Figure 7.4   The distribution of spending preferences in Britain and 32 democracies

local currencies, therefore, this has been transformed into standardized variables for comparison purposes and currency values are not used in Figure 7.5.

Contrary to the assumption in much of the literature that low incomes mean a high demand for spending and high incomes the opposite, there is in fact a non-linear relationship between the demand for spending and income. Both low-income and high-income individuals want less spending, while those in the middle-income categories have the greatest demand for government expenditure. To be fair, this relationship is skewed so that above average and high-income individuals are all less enthusiastic about spending than everyone else except respondents in the lowest income category. The skew means that there is a tendency for the affluent to want less spending than the poor, but the relationship is not a simple one.

Another way of looking at the same relationship is to examine the demand for spending among people in different occupational status categories. Given that middle-class professionals and managers have relatively high incomes and often receive perks such as health benefits and subsidized travel, we might expect them to be less enthusiastic about public spending than manual workers who do not get these benefits. But

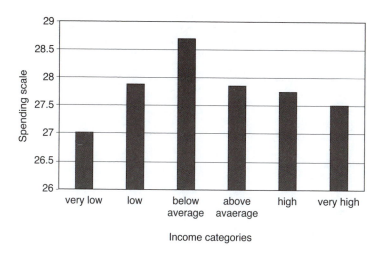

Source: ISSP, *Role of Government Survey*, 2006.

Figure 7.5   The relationship between income and spending preferences in 32 democracies

it turns out that there is no simple relationship between occupational status and attitudes. Individuals in white-collar technical jobs, who are ranked lower in the occupational status scale, are less enthusiastic about spending than their higher-status professional counterparts. On the other hand, semi-skilled and unskilled workers are more supportive of spending than are managers and professionals, consequently, there is something of a relationship between occupational status and the demand for spending, but it is certainly not uniform.

Figure 7.5 shows that income and socio-economic status clearly influence the individual's demand for spending, but this is far from being the whole story. Other factors are at work in explaining why so many individuals want more government spending in so many countries. Clearly, these factors relate to the sociotropic concerns of the type discussed earlier. One of the key sociotropic indicators is individual views about the role of government in society. If a citizen thinks that government should be very highly interventionist in society and carry out much more for its citizens, then they are likely to want more spending. If, on the other, they think that government is too big and interferes too much in the day-to-day lives of its citizens, then they are likely to oppose this.

Table 7.2   Views about the role of government in 32 democracies, 2006

	Definitely should not (%)	Probably should not (%)	Probably should (%)	Definitely should (%)
Provide healthcare for the sick	1	3	28	69
Provide a decent living standard for the elderly	1	4	32	64
Impose strict laws to protect the environment	1	5	38	56
Provide financial help to students	2	7	38	53
Keep prices under § control	4	9	37	50
Help industry to grow	3	14	47	37
Reduce income differences between rich and poor	8	16	33	42
Provide affordable housing	3	12	45	40
Provide a job for everyone who wants one	10	19	33	39
Provide a decent living standard for the unemployed	7	19	44	30

Source: ISSP, *Role of Government Survey*, 2006.

We can examine this idea with the help of the role of government measures discussed in Chapter 2. The same measures for all 32 countries in the survey appear in Table 7.2. We saw in the earlier chapter that there was a strong belief in Britain that the state should provide healthcare and a decent standard of living for the elderly. The same consensus of opinion applies across the 32 countries. But further comparisons between Tables 2.1 and 7.2 show that Britons are distinctly more conservative in their views about the role of government in comparison with the citizens of other countries. This is true in relation to protection of the environment, giving financial assistance to students, keeping prices in check, helping industry to grow, reducing income differences, providing jobs and housing, and also a decent standard of living for the

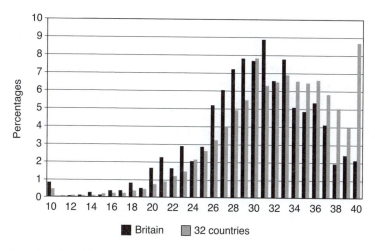

Source: ISSP, *Role of Government Survey*, 2006.

Figure 7.6   The demand for government in Britain and 32 democracies

unemployed. There are some quite marked differences between attitudes in Britain and in the rest of the world.

Again to see this more clearly, we can construct a 'role of government' scale in a similar way to the demand for spending scale. If a respondent says 'definitely should' that scores 4; 'probably should' scores 3; 'probably should not' scores 2; and finally, 'definitely should not' scores 1. The scores for each of the ten items are then cumulated so that a respondent who is against all types of government activity would score 10 and a respondent who is definitely in favour of all types of activities would score 40. The scale can be seen in Figure 7.6 which again compares Britain with the other countries. The two distributions are skewed to the right with many more respondents wanting government intervention than want the opposite. But as the earlier discussion indicates, Britons are more conservative about government intervention than the rest of the world. There is a sizeable group in the 32 countries who feel that government should intervene heavily in all ten policy areas, giving them a maximum score of 40. This group is much smaller in Britain.

It is interesting to examine the relationship between the 'demand for spending' and the 'role of government' scales. The two measures correspond quite closely, so that opponents of government intervention are also opponents of spending, and vice versa. There is none of the ambiguity about the relationship of the type seen in Figure 7.5 which looks at spending and income. In fact, the relationship between these two measures is much stronger than between income and spending, suggesting that political attitudes to the role of government are more important than personal circumstances when it comes to explaining the individual's support for government spending. In other words, sociotropic concerns are rather more important than egocentric concerns.

What do these findings say about the demand for government in the modern world? They suggest that large numbers of the citizens of democratic countries want a large and active state to provide goods and services and to regulate the economy and society. There is not much evidence of support for a dramatic downsizing of government in response to the financial and economic crisis of recent years. In fact, the evidence suggests that any government which sought to make drastic cuts in spending and which tried to abandon whole areas of policy making to the private sector would probably face serious electoral problems.

However, recent evidence suggests that governments which undertake rapid fiscal adjustments in the face of economic crises are not subsequently punished by their electorates (Alesina, Carloni and Lecce, 2010). The argument that spending cuts automatically create electoral problems, therefore, may be too simplistic. If governments can cut while retaining their reputations for economic competence then the electoral consequences might be quite benign if the voters see this as necessary medicine which needs to be taken. On the other hand, if governments lose their reputation for economic competence in the process of making these cuts, this would be a different matter. The best example of the latter happening in Britain was in 1992 when John Major's government was held responsible for Britain's ejection from the European Monetary System on 'Black Wednesday' in September of that year (Clarke, Sanders, Stewart and Whiteley, 2004: 60–1). Voters rapidly concluded that this crisis was the fault of the Conservatives and the party lost its reputation for economic competence, which contributed to the Labour landslide victory in 1997. The party did not subsequently restore its reputation until after David Cameron became the leader in 2005.

Attitudes to taxation are the reverse of attitudes to spending, and Table 7.3 looks at perceptions of the burden of taxation for individuals in different income groups. This is the equivalent of Table 2.5 in Chapter 2 which looked just at Britain. There is a distinct bias in favour of respon-

Table 7.3   Attitudes to taxation in 32 democracies, 2006

Taxes for:	Much too low	Too low	About right	Too high	Much too high
High-income groups	12	31	31	17	9
Middle-income groups	1	4	38	44	14
Low-income groups	1	3	21	39	36

Source: ISSP, *Role of Government Survey*, 2006.

dents believing that taxation is too high in these countries, although there are significant differences between perceptions of the burdens for different income groups. Some 75 per cent of respondents thought that taxation was too high for low-income individuals, compared with only 26 per cent who thought this about high-income individuals.

Once again it is useful to compare Britain with the other countries by constructing a scale of attitudes to taxation. If the responses to the three questions are cumulated an individual who thinks that taxation is too low for all income groups would score 3 and an individual who thought it was too high for all groups would score 15. The scales for Britain and the thirty-two countries appear in Figure 7.7 and they show widespread support for the view that taxes are too high in all countries, and in this case Britons do not differ very much from citizens elsewhere. These perceptions are of course inconsistent with the evidence in Figure 7.3 showing that the public want high levels of public spending. There is clearly a paradox at work with citizens wanting more government intervention and spending while at the same time being reluctant to pay for it with extra taxation. This confirms research showing that there is a 'fiscal illusion' at work in the minds of the public, who have a limited understanding of taxation and government spending, creating imbalances of this type (Winter and Mouritzen, 2001).

We might expect egocentric considerations to influence the relationship between taxation and income, with low-income individuals being less opposed to taxation than high-income individuals. When this relationship is examined it shows that very high-income individuals do indeed believe that taxation is too high across the democratic world. But that aside, there is no clear relationship between attitudes to taxation and income of the type that would exist if individuals were making up their minds solely on the basis of self-interest. If egocentric considerations dominated the picture, then low-income individuals would favour higher taxation and high income individuals would oppose them. Instead we observe no systematic relationship between income and attitudes,

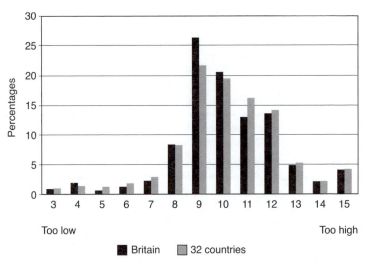

Source: ISSP, *Role of Government Survey*, 2006.

Figure 7.7   Attitudes to taxation in Britain and 32 democracies

apart from the aversion of the high-income group. This undermines the idea that egocentric evaluations are the basis of citizen thinking on taxation.

Attitudes to transfer payments

The discussion up to this point has packaged together a diverse set of spending categories. A key distinction for understanding the growth of government is the fact that there are different types of government spending. There is spending on classic public goods, such as defence, policing and the administration of justice, and these services are provided by all states. If the state did not provide policing and defence then these public goods would be under-provided and much of civilized life would be more challenging. These services are examples of relatively pure public goods.

Pure public goods have the characteristics of jointness of supply, which means that their consumption by one person does not reduce the amount available for others, and also the impossibility of exclusion, in that it is impractical to restrict their use to specific individuals (Samuelson, 1954). These characteristics can be observed in relation to spending on defence. Once the British government provides defence then it is available to everyone in the country and one person's consumption does not detract from that of another. Equally, it is impossible for the government only to defend taxpayers and ignore the rest, so defence cannot be 'sold' only to those people who are willing to pay for it directly.

Once public goods are provided they can be used by all, making it difficult for a commercial organization to profit from them. Without the state, these types of goods would not be adequately provided, and this fact has important implications for the demand for spending. It means that most, if not all, citizens are likely to support government spending on these key public goods and this is true purely on egocentric grounds without taking into account sociotropic considerations. Old people, young people, the rich, the poor, high status and low status individuals all benefit from equal protection before the law and from common defence. For this reason, spending on such things are not likely to be controversial because they go to the heart of the reason why the state exists in the first place. Of course, there may be arguments about how much of these goods should be provided but almost everyone will look to the state to make them available.

The same point cannot be made about transfer payments, which are not public goods but rather 'merit goods' (Musgrave, 1959). These are goods and services provided on the basis of need and not on ability to pay. Merit goods can take the form of education and healthcare, but their most clear-cut manifestation is in the form of transfer payments. The motivation for transfer payments is to reduce social exclusion and protect individuals from the risks and costs arising from unemployment, retirement, health problems and so on. They are designed to alleviate the consequences of inequalities and the risks arising from purely private market provision. Since public goods and transfer payments are rather different forms of public spending, any adequate theory of the demand for government needs to examine them separately. In Table 7.1 there are two examples of such transfer payment, namely, spending on pensions and on unemployment benefits, so it is interesting to focus on the demand for these in particular. They can be aggregated into an 'attitudes to transfer payments' scale.

If we compare attitudes to transfer payments in Britain and in the other thirty-one countries, it reflects what is now becoming a familiar pattern. Britons are clearly more conservative about such payments than their counterparts across the democratic world. The average score on the 10-point scale for Britain is 6.6, whereas across other democratic populations it is 7.3, showing that there is more enthusiasm for pensions and unemployment benefits elsewhere than in Britain.

We observed in Figure 7.5 that there was an ambiguous relationship between attitudes to spending and income, suggesting that the common assumption that low-income individuals want more spending and high-income individuals want the opposite is not accurate. Again we can examine the relationship between the transfer payments scale in income in Britain and in other countries. In the case of Britain, low-income individuals are more supportive of transfer payments than high-income individuals. The effects are not strong, but clearly the assumed relationship between income and spending referred to earlier works better with transfer payments than it does with spending in general. This is not true for other democracies however, where above-average-income individuals are more supportive of transfer payments than below-average-income individuals.

Overall, this evidence suggests that egocentric considerations play a role in moulding attitudes to public spending across the democratic world, and have their most important effects in relation to transfer payments such as pensions and social benefits in Britain. For this kind of public spending affluent citizens are rather less enthusiastic about it than poor citizens, something which is much less true of public spending in general, particularly spending on public goods such as police and defence. However, there is still a puzzle to answer: Why don't poor people want more spending? We examine this issue next.

The demand for government spending and income

The ambiguous relationship between income and the demand for government spending was apparent in Figure 7.5. This raises a puzzle: why should low income people be averse to government spending, particularly on transfer payments which might directly benefit them? The answer to this lies in the fact that the demand for spending is influenced by other factors as well as income and perceptions of the role of government discussed earlier.

To see how this works it is necessary to consider what people are being asked to do when they are questioned about government spending and taxation. Government is a complex activity and, as we have already mentioned, there is no simple relationship between taxation and spending. It is hard for individuals to work out if they are likely to benefit or to lose from additional spending and taxation. It is even more difficult to work this out for people who lack a basic understanding of the workings of government and who feel that they are unable to influence what happens. Thus efficacy, or the feeling that an individual understands government and politics and can make a difference to outcomes, is likely to play an important role in affecting how they see government and public spending. If people have a very limited understanding of how politics works and they do not feel that they can influence what happens then they are not likely to attach a great deal of weight to government policies, even those that may, in theory, benefit them.

We have discussed the topic of political efficacy in a previous chapter and it is noteworthy that there is a relationship between efficacy and individual incomes in the Role of Government Survey. When asked to respond to the statement: 'People like me have no say in what government does', some 62 per cent of respondents in the very low-income category agreed or strongly agreed with the statement, compared with only 44 per cent in the very high-income group. As one moves up the income scale respondents are less likely to agree with the statement. Not surprisingly people with low incomes and low status in society feel disempowered. Since it is hard to become enthusiastic about something you don't really understand or feel you can influence, it is not surprising that low-income people are less supportive of government spending.

Another question in the survey which speaks to the same issue asks respondents if there is anyone they know who could influence an important decision in their favour. In effect, this is a rough measure of their perceptions of efficacy in relation to the wider society, and not just government. In an influential article Granovetter (1973) explained that 'weak ties' are quite important to individuals. These are networks of acquaintances who are not family members or friends but who can be approached to obtain useful information, favours and inside knowledge about jobs, benefits and other things. In effect they are a type of social capital which can be utilized by individuals to promote their interests. An extensive network of weak ties allows individuals to exert influence over their lives in a way which is very difficult for someone who lacks those ties.

In the event, there is a strong relationship between income and perceptions of weak ties, which is captured by the question on people influencing decisions on their behalf. Some 47 per cent of people in the very low-income category said that they had nobody who could influence a decision in their favour. This compares with 29 per cent of people in the very high-income category. At the other end of the scale close to 30 per cent of people in the very high-income category thought that there were some or a lot of people who could do this, compared with only 17 per cent of the very low-income category. Once again, further up the income scale the perception that individuals can draw on social ties to influence a decision in their favour grows stronger.

Conclusion

This chapter has examined the demand for government from a comparative perspective and it shows that Britain is not in the forefront of demanding state intervention and additional spending in comparison with other advanced countries. On the other hand, it is fairly clear that the government has grown over time, both in Britain and elsewhere and this reflects the fact that there is a strong demand for government intervention in the economy and in society in contemporary democracies. Bureaucratic rent-seeking may play a minor role in this and the expansion of the franchise is a background factor which may have contributed to it, but ultimately the state has grown because citizens want it. They value protection from the risks associated with private market provision at different stages of their lives and support social protection because it helps them to deal with the uncertainties associated with modern society. Since many of these risks are not covered by private markets, which often fail to deliver an adequate supply of merit goods, quite apart from public goods, citizens demand that the state steps in to do this.

The chapter started out by asking the question: Is the state too big? Following the recent economic crisis this issue has moved up the agenda as never before, and in Britain the coalition government is determined to address the issue. However, the strength of support for state spending and state intervention demonstrates the electoral risks for any government seeking to substantially reduce the size of the state. If a government withdraws benefits from claimants, eliminates public services and reduces employment opportunities by cutting the public sector it is playing a very risky electoral game. There is a good reason why neither Margaret Thatcher nor Ronald Reagan were able to reduce the size of the state despite being ideologically strongly committed to this policy. It is because a serious programme of cuts in state services is unlikely to be acceptable to citizens in general, who will respond to it by voting out a government which attempts it.

Having examined the different dimensions of citizenship in the early chapters of this book, in the next chapter we change the focus of the discussion to pose the questions: What difference does it make? What is the relationship between governance and citizenship? We consider this issue next.

8

Government Effectiveness and Civil Society

We have been looking closely at the values and practices which make up civil society and have seen that voluntary activity, institutions, such as political parties and norms, which support civic engagement and obedience to the law are all important ingredients in civic culture. But does a healthy civil society make for effective government? This is a crucial question, first raised in empirical research by Almond and Verba in their landmark study in the 1960s (Almond and Verba, 1963). They argued that a civic culture was crucial to understanding and explaining effective government.

In this chapter we focus closely on the relationship between civil society and the effectiveness of government. The chapter starts with a discussion of what is actually meant by government effectiveness, and how such a concept can be measured. This leads into an examination of the relationship between government effectiveness and some of the key indicators of civil society examined earlier. Much as in Chapter 7, this is a comparative analysis since the only way effectively to study the relationship between civil society and governance is by comparing Britain with other countries. We need to observe variations in both civil society and in government effectiveness across different states to understand relationships.

What is government effectiveness?

Put simply, most people would argue that an effective government is one that delivers what its citizens want. That is to say, such a government will provide efficient public services such as healthcare, social benefits and education; it will keep the streets relatively safe from crime and disorder; it will protect its citizens from terrorist attacks; it will collect taxes effectively and spend the money efficiently; it will listen to its citizens and be responsive to their concerns; and finally, it will be free of corruption and will control the special interests which try to use the state for their own benefit. In short, government effectiveness is a multi-dimensional concept, which touches on all aspects of the relationship between citizens and the state.

For some years, researchers at the World Bank have been working on the problem of understanding governance as part of their brief to understand and promote economic development across the world. In their analysis they define good governance in terms of six interrelated dimensions (Kaufmann, Kray and Mastruzzi, 2006: 4):

- *Voice and accountability*: the extent to which a country's citizens are able to participate in selecting their government, as well as freedom of expression, freedom of association, and free media;
- *Political stability and absence of violence*: perceptions of the likelihood that the government will be destabilized or overthrown by unconstitutional or violent means, including political violence and terrorism;
- *Government effectiveness* the quality of public services, the quality of the civil service and the degree of its independence from political pressure, the quality of policy formulation and implementation, and the credibility of the government's commitment to such policies;
- *Regulatory quality*: the ability of the government to formulate and implement sound policies and regulations that permit and promote private sector development;
- *Rule of law* the extent to which agents have confidence in, and abide by the rules of, society and, in particular, the quality of contact enforcement, the police and the courts, as well as the likelihood of crime and violence;
- *Control of corruption* the extent to which public power is exercised for private gain, including both petty and grand forms of corruption, as well as 'capture' of the state by elites and private interests.

The measures used to define these six governance indicators are based on several-hundred variables measuring perceptions of governance, drawn from 31 separate data sources constructed by 25 different organizations (Kaufmann, Kray and Mastruzzi, 2006: 1). The Bank uses a sophisticated statistical algorithm to combine the data from these diverse sources into broadly defined measures. It can be seen that their approach combines indicators of civil society, such as participation and freedom of expression, with measures of government delivery, such as regulation and policy implementation. In other words, they are defining good government both in terms of the effectiveness of civil society as well as in

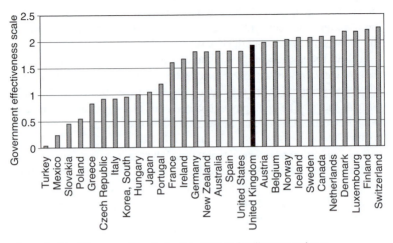

Source: Quality of Governance Cross-Section Data, 2005; see http://www.qog.pol.gu.se.

Figure 8.1   Government effectiveness in OECD countries, 2005

relation to the efficiency of policy delivery. The World Bank's remit is to look at all types of government across the world at all stages of economic and political development with the aim of promoting prosperity. But this definition is too wide for our purposes, since we are focusing on government effectiveness in advanced industrial societies, such as Britain. In these countries, corruption may exist but the problem is relatively small in comparison with some developing nations in Asia and Africa. Similarly, the rule of law works with varying degrees of efficiency in different countries but it has only broken down and become a huge problem in a limited number of failed states. It is, for the most part, not a serious problem in OECD countries.

Therefore, to apply the World Bank theoretical framework to the task of understanding governance in the advanced industrial democracies, it is necessary to separate out the measures of civil society and government effectiveness. It is also important to focus closely on what really defines effectiveness. Accordingly, the primary focus of this chapter is on the World Bank's 'government effectiveness' measure, which as the earlier discussion indicates largely relates to the quality of public services and the efficiency of the policy-making process. The scores for the thirty OECD countries on the government effectiveness scale in 2005 appear in Figure 8.1.

The figure shows that there is a wide variation in the effectiveness of governments among OECD countries. The least effective government was Turkey and the most effective one was Switzerland. Britain appears twelfth in the list, below Scandinavian countries but above countries such as Italy and France. It appears that Britain is fairly close to the United States in terms of the effectiveness measure. There is an interesting north–south distinction in the data with the Nordic countries such as Denmark and Sweden scoring highly and the southern European countries such as Portugal, Italy and Greece doing much less well. To place this in an international context, however, all of the OECD countries have positive scores on the scale, but if we look beyond these countries to Africa and Asia there are many countries with negative scores. It appears, therefore, that the OECD countries, as a whole, are among the most well governed in the world.

Government effectiveness and civil society

The relationship between civil society and governance has been widely discussed in the literature (Dahl, 1971; Lijphart, 1977; Przeworski, 1991; Putnam, 1993). However, it is not at all obvious that an active civil society will necessarily produce good governance in all circumstances. For example, very high levels of political participation may have a negative influence on effective governance. One can think of scenarios in which widespread protest behaviour, for example, as occurred in France in 1968 and again in Britain during the poll-tax riots of the late 1980s, might paralyse decision making, and thus undermine government effectiveness. Similarly, a norm that supports public 'voice' as a desirable thing in the policy-making process might make decision making very difficult if everyone gives voice at the same time. Thus it is important to examine how civil society and government effectiveness are related in practice.

We will examine the effectiveness of government in relation to three aspects of civil society. First, there is the relationship between civic attitudes, values and effectiveness, which was discussed extensively in Chapter 2. That chapter examined a variety of attitudinal indicators which contribute to civil society such as tolerance, efficacy and interest in politics. It was suggested that at the core of civil society is the relationship between the state and its citizens, with the latter demanding benefits from government in exchange for giving support to the state by paying taxes and obeying the law. In that discussion, we focused closely on this relationship, looking at the demand for government on the one hand and the willingness of citizens to pay taxes on the other. We would expect societies in which there was a balance between expectations of government and the recognition of obligations by citizens to have fairly effective governments.

The second aspect of civil society, explored in Chapter 3, is political participation. That chapter looked at electoral turnout in addition to other measures of political participation such as boycotting goods, protesting and being active in a political organization. Political participation is important since it gives expression to what people want from government and helps to give legitimacy to the state. Elections involve a choice between broad directions in which governments can travel, and these are set out in summary form in the rival party manifestos. Citizens are endorsing a strategy for future governance when they vote, and this is at the core of the mandate theory of government. In addition, when citizens lobby their elected representatives, demonstrate over issues they feel strongly about, or buy fair trade goods, they are signalling what they want from government. Equally, when one party wins the election that adds legitimacy to its programme for governance, so that citizens will recognize and accept the policy changes that a new government can bring about. Accordingly, the efficient signalling of citizen demands and the legitimization of policy programmes should improve government effectiveness.

The organizational dimension of civil society in the form of political parties was examined in Chapter 4, covering both local and parliamentary levels. More generally, government is supported by institutions such as parties, interest groups and voluntary organizations, which play an important role in translating citizen demands into policy proposals and also in legitimizing decision making. Therefore, the relationship between the effectiveness of such institutions and that of government is the third broad issue to be examined in this chapter. The argument is that when institutions such as political parties work well, both at the grassroots and at the parliamentary levels, this should improve the effectiveness of government.

The discussion of social capital in Chapter 6 broadened the analysis of attitudes and organizations by looking at interpersonal trust and volunteering, arguing that these make a major contribution to civil society. Social capital combines attitudes, participation and institutions into one broad overarching theme. To reiterate points made earlier, social capital greatly facilitates collective action in which citizens have to work together to solve problems by fostering interpersonal trust. If people are willing to work together because they trust each other, this should make the task of governing much easier and more effective. If individuals trust their governments they should be willing to listen to them and be persuaded that changes in behaviour are necessary. On the other hand, a lack of trust indicates that governments will have to rely on coercion and sanctions to change behaviour, which are much less effective. A lack of trust in government also means that large numbers of citizens will devote their time and efforts to ignoring or circumventing govern- ment actions. This point is best illustrated in relation to taxation; if taxes are increased beyond a certain level then the total revenue falls rather than increases, because people spend a lot more time and effort avoiding payments, either by legal or illegal means (Slemrod and Bakija, 2004).

All these points relate to the links between civil society and govern- ment and they will be examined below. But there is an alternative expla- nation of the effectiveness of government which rivals that of civil society. It may be argued that government effectiveness is merely a reflection of the effectiveness of the wider society. If a society is rich, highly developed, well-educated and its citizens enjoy a high degree of equality, then government will work well simply because society works well. If on the other hand, society is poor, uneducated, under-developed and has high levels of inequality then government will be ineffective because society works badly. This argument is not inconsistent with the idea that civil society matters for government, it just implies that the explanation of the sources of effective government is deeply rooted in society, rather than in political participation or in social norms and values. If so, broad characteristics such as the wealth, fairness and effi- ciency of a society are likely to be more fundamental than civic values and practices, since the latter are only a reflection of the former. To explore this idea further, it is useful to look at a measure of human devel- opment which may explain many of the differences between countries in government effectiveness observed in Figure 8.1.

Empirical evidence on civil society and governance

The key factors discussed in Chapter 5 were public perceptions of the government's responsibility for delivering various goods and services, and also the citizen's sense of obligations that they should pay their taxes and obey the law. To explore the links between these measures and government effectiveness we again use the World Values Survey (Inglehart, 1997). The World Values Survey has data on these measures for all thirty OECD countries, unlike the Role of Government Survey examined in the previous chapter which excludes a number of these countries. However, the World Values Survey is more limited in its coverage of indicators of civil society compared with the Role of Government Survey, but there are enough measures to explore the links between civil society and effective government for our purposes.

One question in the World Values Survey asked respondents if they felt that government should take more responsibility for ensuring that everyone is provided for in their particular country. In effect, this is a broad measure of the demand for government. The responses are measured using a ten-point scale, where a low score indicates respondents feel that the government should do more, and high scores that they feel it should do less and people should provide for themselves. The average score on this measure for each country can be compared with the government effectiveness scale. The relationship between these two measures in the OECD countries appears in Figure 8.2.

Figure 8.2 is known as a scattergram with each of the diamonds in the diagram representing the average scores on the two variables in a given country. It is readily apparent that there is a relationship between the two measures so that government is more effective in countries where citizens believe that the state should do more for its citizens. The summary regression line shows that there is a downward sloping relationship between these variables and a fairly strong correlation of -0.57 between them. Thus the government is more effective in societies where people think that government should take more responsibility for policy delivery. Britain is highlighted in the diagram and is located towards the interventionist end of the spectrum rather than the *laissez-faire* end with respect to the demand for government and, as we saw in Figure 8.1, it is in the middle of the range of scores on government effectiveness. Of course, the causal relationship between the two measures is ambiguous. It is possible that if citizens want more from their governments, that will produce an improvement in performance, or it could be that an improvement in performance makes people want more government, or it could be a combination of both. But insofar as attitudes to government intervention in society are a good indicator of a civil society, the figure shows that the greater the demand for intervention the more effective government is likely to be.

As the discussion in Chapter 2 indicated, another aspect of the demand for government is the citizen's sense of obligation to society. There is a question in the World Values Survey, which asks if cheating on taxes is ever justifiable. Again this is measured with a ten-point scale

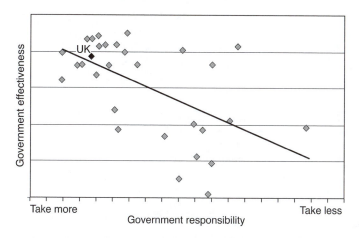

Source: Quality of Governance Cross-Section Data, 2005; see http://www.qog.pol.gu.se.

Figure 8.2   The relationship between government effectiveness and perceptions of government responsibility in OECD countries (correlation = −0.57)

with a low score denoting that cheating is never justified and a high score indicating the opposite. However, in this case the relationship between the two measures in the OECD countries is weak and not statistically significant. We cannot be sure that any relationship exists between the variables, so norms about taxation do not appear to reinforce good governance. However, this conclusion should be modified somewhat, since the great majority of people in these countries think that cheating on taxes is never justified, so there is not much variation in the scale across the advanced countries in the OECD. Thus it is possible that the measure does not adequately discriminate between countries because of the broad consensus. This fact may explain why attitudes to taxation appear to be unrelated to government effectiveness.

Up to this point we have been examining the relationship between norms and government effectiveness. Turning next to the relationship between political participation and government effectiveness, this relationship is summarized in Figure 8.3. Chapter 3 explored different forms of participation and the World Values data makes it possible to construct an index of political action from a battery of participation items. These items first appeared in one the earliest comparative surveys of political participation (see Barnes, Kaase *et al.*, 1979). Respondents were asked

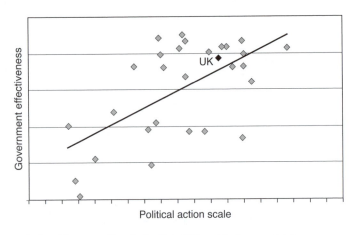

Source: Quality of Governance Cross-Section Data, 2005; see http://www.qog.pol.gu.se.

Figure 8.3　The relationship between government effectiveness and the political action scale in OECD countries (correlation = 0.62)

how many of the following activities they had undertaken: signing a petition, joining a boycott, attending a demonstration, joining an unofficial strike and occupying buildings or factories. The relationship between government effectiveness and the average scores on this action scale appears in Figure 8.3. This relationship is quite strong showing that countries with high levels of political participation also have effective governments. The participation scale does not include electoral turnout, but this is also related to effectiveness. The correlation between turnout in the most recent national election and government effectiveness was +0.39. As we have suggested, turnout helps to legitimate government so it is not surprising that government works better in countries where many people vote.

Chapter 4 showed that political parties were the most important institution of civil society. In the World Values Survey, respondents were asked how much confidence they had in parties in their country with a low score denoting a complete lack of confidence and a high score denoting a great deal of confidence. The correlation between confidence in political parties and government effectiveness is +0.66 which is quite strong, suggesting that if political parties are thought to work well then the government works well too.

Another theme in Chapter 4 was the role of parties in Parliament, and the relationship between confidence in Parliament and government effectiveness is of considerable interest. The confidence in Parliament measure provides an indirect indicator of the effectiveness of parties at the parliamentary level, with the assumption being that if parties do not work very well at the parliamentary level then the institution itself will not work well either. This is the strongest relationship between any of the measures we have been looking at up to this point, with a correlation of +0.72. Perhaps, not surprisingly, public confidence in a country's legislature plays a very important role in influencing the effectiveness of its government.

It is not difficult to work out why confidence in Parliament is so closely associated with government effectiveness. The legislature is the focus of political activity in almost all democratic countries. It is the core institution in which national debates about politics and policy making take place and to which the average citizen and the media look to when they are trying to make sense of politics or when they want the state to deal with social problems. If citizens lack confidence in their legislature then it is hard for the government and the policy-making process to be effective.

The discussion of social capital in Chapter 5 focused on voluntary activities and also on interpersonal trust as measures of this concept. In the World Values Survey, interpersonal trust was measured using the following question: 'Generally speaking, would you say that most people can be trusted or that you need to be very careful in dealing with people?' Respondents who agreed that most people can be trusted scored one and the rest scored zero. If the scores are averaged for each country there is a strong relationship between these scores and government effectiveness in these countries with a correlation of +0.67. This indicates that government is much more effective in countries where the citizens trust each other, compared with countries where trust is weak. It is also the case that voluntary activity and government effectiveness are related, with a correlation of +0.57 between membership of a voluntary organization and effectiveness. Both of these reinforce the conclusion that social capital is an important factor in explaining effective policy making and good governance. The evidence up to this point suggests that civil society and effective government are closely related in many different ways. Countries experiencing high levels of participation, together with strong norms stressing the importance of being a good citizen, volunteering and taking an active role in society, are also those which have effective governments.

However, it was also suggested earlier that a benign civil society and an effective government may just be a reflection of deeper and more fundamental forces in society. These relate to living standards, equality of opportunity and outcomes, as well as to the overall well-being of society. If so, the relationship between civil society and governance may merely be a reflection of these deeper forces rather than an important phenomenon in its own right. The most obvious and general determinant is how wealthy a country is, since a high Gross Domestic Product means that governments are able to take a variety of actions, which would be difficult or impossible in a poorer society. Nonetheless, the relationship between government effectiveness and GDP per capita, that is the standard of living of citizens in these countries, is very strong with a correlation of +0.76. Not surprisingly, prosperous societies have very successful governments, although once again the causal relationship is ambiguous; prosperity can cause good government, but the process may also work in reverse.

While prosperity is desirable, inequality is not, and so it is interesting to examine the relationship between income inequality and government effectiveness across the set of countries. The Gini coefficient is the most widely accepted measure of inequality and it identifies the extent to which income is concentrated in a few hands. There is a negative correlation of -0.42 between the Gini coefficient and government effectiveness, the more unequal the society the less effective is the government. Note that this relationship is not as strong as that between national income and effective governance, but it is nonetheless significant.

Perhaps the broadest measure of the social characteristics of a country is provided by the Human Development Index (HDI). This is a composite measure of the performance of a country in relation to three basic dimensions of human development, namely, health, knowledge and prosperity (see http://hdr.undp.org). In constructing the index, health is measured by life expectancy at birth, knowledge by the adult literacy rate together with enrolments in primary, secondary and tertiary education, and finally, prosperity as measured by GDP per capita. Thus the HDI combines broad measures of the 'success' of society in looking after its people and promoting their welfare. The relationship between the HDI and government effectiveness is the strongest one seen so far in this chapter with a correlation of +0.88. To be fair, the human development index is a very broad measure and as we saw earlier, the government effectiveness scale is quite broad too, and so both measures are drawing on similar data in their construction. Notwithstanding this point, it is interesting that government effectiveness has such a pervasive impact on the well-being of citizens in society.

Up to this point, we have observed a number of relationships between government effectiveness and indicators of civil society, such as norms, attitudes and behaviour. This approach has been illuminating but it says little about which are the most important factors in explaining effectiveness. In particular, it does not discriminate between the indicators of civil society and the broader measures such as GDP and the HDI. To do this we require a multivariate analysis which will be examined in the next section.

What is important – civil society or human development?

To address the issue of what are the most important factors for explaining effective government, it is necessary to analyse all the relevant variables together rather than just looking at them two at a time. This can be done with a multiple regression analysis and this is explained informally here. This technique makes it possible to identify the unique contribution of each factor to good government, while at the same time taking into account the influence of other factors. For example, it will tell us the relationship between GDP and government effectiveness while taking into account the role of political participation, confidence in political parties and the other measures. Clearly, separating out the important links in this way is the best way to find out if effectiveness is driven by the efficiency of the society as a whole or by political participation and social norms.

To categorize these relationships we use the strongest measures of the relationships examined in the earlier chapters such as norms and attitudes and political participation and relate them to government effectiveness. Thus perception of government responsibility for delivering benefits examined in Figure 8.2 was the most important factor in delivering effective government in the discussion of attitudes and values. Similarly, the political action scale which appears in Figure 8.3 was the most highly correlated measure of political participation with government effectiveness, in relation to the discussion of Chapter 3. In addition, confidence in Parliament showed the importance of institutions examined originally in Chapter 4 and interpersonal trust shows the relevance of social capital from the discussion in Chapter 5. Finally, as mentioned earlier, the HDI is the broadest and most important measure of development and it had the highest correlation with government effectiveness of the social structural indicators.

Figure 8.4 measures the impact of the different variables on government effectiveness arising from a multivariate regression model. The columns in the figure represent the size of the correlations

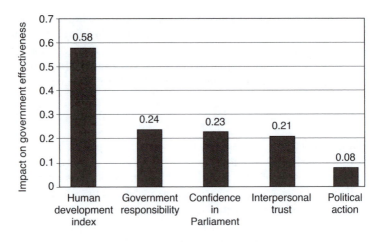

Source: Quality of Governance Cross-Section Data, 2005; see http://www.qog.pol.gu.se.

Figure 8.4   The impact of civil society and the HDI on government effectiveness in OECD countries

between the measure and government effectiveness, taking into account the influence of the other variables in the model. In other words, the correlation between the human development index and government effectiveness is 0.58 when the effects of trust, political action, confidence in Parliament and perceptions of government responsibility are taken into account. This is significantly smaller than the correlation of 0.88 mentioned earlier, which ignored the influence of these other variables.

The results in Figure 8.4 show that the HDI is the most important factor for influencing government effectiveness, and it stands out as being significantly stronger than the other variables. Not surprisingly, fundamental characteristics of society such as the health, prosperity and levels of education of the population are really important to good governance. However, a key finding in the figure is that such characteristics are not the only things that matter in explaining good governance because there are significant effects associated with other variables as well. Thus the demand for government, interpersonal trust and confidence in Parliament are all significantly related to government effectiveness alongside the human development index. These findings are important, because they show that measures of civil society matter when

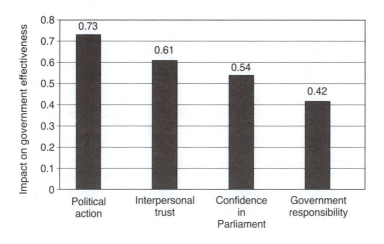

Source: Quality of Governance Cross-Section Data, 2005; see http://www.qog.pol.gu.se.

Figure 8.5   The impact of the HDI on indicators of civil society in OECD countries

it comes to understanding governance. It is not just about how well a society works in terms of looking after its people, but also how active and supportive these people are, which makes government effective.

As the earlier discussion indicated, the HDI captures a broad measure of economic and social development of a society. But if this influences effective governance, it is likely to influence the measures of participation and the indicators of values and attitudes as well. Given that, it is interesting to see how it relates to the various measures of civil society. As Figure 8.4 shows it has a direct effect on governance, but it also has an indirect effect on governance via the measures of civil society. This explains the evidence in Figure 8.5 which shows the correlations between the civil society measures and the HDI arising from a multiple regression analysis. Interestingly enough, the largest correlation is between HDI and the political action index, so that a healthy, educated and prosperous population are quite likely to become involved in politics. This is consistent with the civic voluntarism model of political participation, indicating that high income and well resourced individuals are more likely to participate than their low income, poorly resourced neighbours (see Verba, Schlozman and Brady, 1995). This is true at the country level as well as at the individual level.

A second strong correlation in Figure 8.5 is between HDI and inter-personal trust, the measure of social capital. Researchers on the topic of social capital such as Putnam (1993) are at pains to point out that social capital is not the same as affluence, and indeed in the United States some rich communities have significantly less social capital than poorer communities (Putnam, 2000). While this is certainly true, it also apparent that social capital and high levels of human development go side by side in the advanced industrial countries.

The relationship between the HDI and confidence in Parliament is also quite strong indicating that broad social and economic development directly impacts the effectiveness of this key institution of government. By implication, legislatures, political parties, interest groups and other institutions for governing and giving voice to citizens are likely to work better in healthy, educated and affluent communities. Finally, there is a clear relationship between HDI and perceptions that government should take responsibility for citizen welfare. One view is that countries in which there is a strong demand for government intervention in relation to health, education and welfare, are also the countries which success-fully deliver these services to their populations. Equally, when countries do successfully deliver such policies to their citizens, this brings a greater demand for these services because they are popular and have the support of the voters. In other words, there may be a virtuous circle at work in the relationship between the economic and social character-istics of a society and the effectiveness of its government.

Conclusion

The aim of this chapter has been to bring together evidence linking civil society to the effectiveness and efficiency of government in delivering goods and services. The latter is a key outcome variable in politics, since an efficient policy-making process, which delivers effective policies, is central to good government. The conclusions from the analysis are fairly unequivocal, in that a healthy civil society is strongly linked to an effec-tive government. It is also true that the fundamental characteristics of a society, such as its standard of living, the provision of education for its workforce and the health of its citizens, are very important in explaining good governance. But they are far from being the whole story. It is pos-sible to have an affluent society with an educated workforce which has a rather weak civil society, lacking norms about the importance of gov-ernment and the trustworthiness of fellow citizens. Such a society would

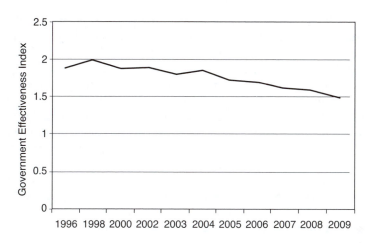

Source: Quality of Governance Data, 2010; see http://www.qog.pol.gu.se.

Figure 8.6   Trends in the government effectiveness index in Britain, 1996–2009

have a less efficient government than it could otherwise achieve if participation were healthy and social norms supportive of effective government were strong.

The discussion in previous chapters has shown that although the civic culture in Britain remains strong it appears to be weakening over time. In Chapter 2, we observed that the demand for government was generally declining and citizens were more inclined to seek their own private solutions to the problems and uncertainties of modern life. Similarly, in Chapter 3, we observed the decline in political participation, particularly electoral participation which has been taking place over the post-war period. The discussion of institutions showed that while political parties are still very important, grassroots activism has declined to a great extent, and the cohesion of parties in Parliament has weakened as well. Finally, Chapter 5 suggested that early optimism that Britain has avoided the decline in social capital which has occurred in the United States is misplaced. It appears that both voluntary activity and interpersonal trust, the key measures of social capital, have also declined. Overall, the picture is one of a weakening civic culture and, following the analysis of this chapter, should imply a decline, over time, in government effectiveness.

Figure 8.6 charts changes in the government effectiveness index for Britain from 1996, when it was first published, up to 2009. It is apparent that the effectiveness of British government has been declining over this period., This is exactly what we would expect if the civic culture, which contributes to the effectiveness of government is also in decline. It should be said that this conclusion is tentative, however, since thirteen years is not a long period over which to judge trends in something that is likely to change slowly and there are uncertainties associated with the World Bank estimates of government effectiveness. However, Figure 8.6 speaks for itself, since the effectiveness of British government declined in all but two of the observations in the dataset. The chances of this happening if effectiveness has not actually declined in practice are pretty small.

It therefore appears that the trends in the civic culture discussed in the earlier chapters of this book are already undermining the effectiveness of British government, and weakening the case for a more interventionist government in the future. Looking back over the post-war years, the 1940s and early 1950s represented the high water mark of government intervention in the economy and in industry. In that period, governments rationed goods, conscripted labour, owned and controlled large areas of industry including coal, steel, power generation, telecommunications, road haulage, water and sewage. They also tightly controlled credit and many prices. One interpretation of the history of the post-war period is that of government retreating from economic intervention by policies of privatization and de-regulation. This has not happened in relation to welfare provision, that is, education, healthcare, and social benefits, but we may be facing such a retreat in the future if the effectiveness of government continues to decline. We have discussed virtuous circles in the relationship between government effectiveness and civil society, but there is also the possibility of vicious circles with declining performance associated with a weakening civil society. If this occurs it could produce a withdrawal of the state from welfare provision, so in the next and final chapter we examine this issue in detail.

9

Civil Society and Governance in the Future

This book has charted the ingredients of the civic culture and civil society in Britain by looking at attitudes, values, participation and also at key institutions such as political parties and Parliament. In this final chapter, we bring it all together by examining, more generally, the links between the various components of civil society, governance and the state of British democracy. Britain is one of the world's oldest democracies and has the 'Mother of Parliaments', but how is contemporary British democracy actually performing? In particular how exactly does democracy relate to civil society? And how can democracy be reinforced and strengthened in the future? To address these questions we need to spell out a broad definition of democracy and then observe how the components of civil society relate to it. Once again this is done using a comparative analysis in order to characterize British democracy in relation to other countries across the advanced industrial world.

The chapter starts by examining what we mean by democracy and also how it should be measured. This leads into a discussion of the relationship between democracy, civic culture and civil society. Subsequently, after examining the state of democracy in Britain, the focus narrows to look closely at the relationship between civil society and welfare provision. This is done in order to explore the 'invisible handshake' or the relationship between citizen demands for policies and their perceptions of obligations to society discussed previously. The story in this book has been a relatively pessimistic one, suggesting that civil society has been weakening in Britain over time and that as a consequence social capital and the effectiveness of government have been declining too. Given this, the latter part of the chapter will focus on what can be done to turn this around and revive civil society in the future.

An important question relates to the role of government in all of this. Is government an obstacle to, or a facilitator in, the task of building civil society? Addressing this issue involves examining the relationship between government and the effectiveness of civil society in a comparative context. Reviving civil society means fostering civic values, promoting participation, and reviving institutions such as Parliament. Most people would agree that reviving these institutions and values is a good idea, but the key question is, can it be done? The discussion will highlight some of the actions that government can take, and then towards the end of the chapter we will examine an important underlying factor, the rise in inequality, which underpins many of these developments.

Shortly after the general election of 2010, the new Coalition government embarked on an ambitious programme of rebuilding civic values called the 'Big Society'. Prime Minister David Cameron endorsed this idea and enthusiastically argued for greater local engagement in delivering services and helping to foster community action. In a speech he argued that voluntary groups 'should be able to run post offices, libraries, transport services and shape housing projects' (Cameron, 2010). His declared aim was to bring about 'the biggest, most dramatic redistribution of power from elites in Whitehall to the man and woman in the street' (Cameron, 2010). Thus, the overall goal of the Big Society is to give individuals and communities greater control over their lives. Clearly, it is important to try to evaluate this initiative in the light of the trends examined earlier.

A central concern is the role of government in helping to bring about the 'Big Society'. From one point of view, government is the problem and not the solution, since it can be argued that the state needs to shrink if room is to be found for greater local autonomy and private initiative. Described as the 'substitute' theory of government, this is the idea that the state needs to downsize in order to stop 'crowding out' voluntary initiatives at the local level. But there is another perspective, or 'complementary' theory, which argues that government is essential for facilitating voluntary action if local initiatives are to be successful. These alternative perspectives will be discussed in the latter part of the chapter, but we begin by examining the links between democracy and civil society.

Democracy, governance and civil society

Despite being the focus of attention of political theorists since the time of the Ancient Greeks, there is no universally agreed definition of democracy. The idea of democracy emerged from the Greek city states, notably Athens, around two-and-a-half-thousand years ago, and was codified by Plato, Aristotle and Thucydides who wrote about the history and problems of governance in these states. At the heart of their conception of democracy is the idea that those who own and control property should collectively create and enforce the laws which determine how such property is disposed. Thus democracy meant citizens acting as self-governing stakeholders, and is in sharp contrast to the conception of citizenship in authoritarian states which sees the individual as a subject of the ruler (Clarke, 1996).

Much has been written about contemporary conceptions of democracy (Lijphart, 1977; Barber, 1984; Bobbio, 1989; Dahl, 1956; Dunn, 1992; Held, 1996). In particular, Held (1996) spells out rival conceptions of democracy associated with republican, liberal and Marxist thought and examines how these have gradually developed from classical notions. One particular theorist, Robert Dahl, has been influential in the empirical analysis of contemporary democracy (1971, 1989). Dahl adopts the term polyarchy to describe contemporary representative democracy. In a polyarchy, full-time representatives make decisions and ordinary citizens play a relatively minor role in the day-to-day government of the state.

Dahl characterizes polyarchy as having eight distinct features as far as its citizens are concerned. These are the right to vote; the right to seek public office; the right to compete with other candidates for votes; free and fair elections, freedom of assembly and the right to join parties and other political organizations; freedom of speech; media diversity; and government policies which reflect the preferences of citizens. This appears to be a very broad concept of democracy, but despite that it has little to say about the processes of government itself, about the resources that different citizens bring to the task of participating in the democratic process, or about political culture in general.

Przeworski (1991) highlights the importance of resources as well as institutions in his discussion of emerging democracies in the modern world. His analysis recognizes that differences in income, social class, and access to influence and life chances all play a key role in the democratic process. As he explains, 'If democratic institutions are universalistic – blind to the identity of the participants – those with greater resources are more likely to win conflicts' (Przeworski, 1991: 11). This is a broader definition of democracy than Dahl's, which goes beyond the institutions associated with elections and representation that are the focus of Dahl's analysis. More specifically, from Przeworski's perspective, market power plays a key role in influencing the processes and outcomes of democratic practices.

Contemporary accounts have broadened the concept of democracy in order to incorporate many more features that are relevant for understanding the modern democratic state. For example, Kekic (2007) defines democracy in terms of five attributes: free and fair elections, effective civil liberties, a functioning and responsive government, a supportive political culture and widespread political participation. His approach focuses on both defining and measuring democracy. Much as is true for the World Bank's Governance indicators, this definition combines measures of civil society, governance, the policy-making process and political culture. Kekic (2007) reports on the Economist Intelligence Unit's index of democracy, which provides a snapshot of the current state of democracy in 165 nations, just short of the entire population of the world. The report classifies countries into 'full democracies', 'flawed democracies'; 'hybrid regimes' and 'authoritarian regimes'. As we shall see subsequently, Britain appears at the lower end of the full democracy category.

Clearly, to understand how civil society interacts with democracy and governance it is important to take into account a broad conception of democracy. The Economist Intelligence Unit's index of democracy is based on a total of 60 different indicators categorized into the five groups. The data is based on expert judgements, opinion research and electoral data. The five groups are: *electoral processes and pluralism*, which measures free and fair elections; *civil liberties* which captures freedom of speech, the press, religion, freedom of association and a fair judicial process; the *functioning of government*, which relates to control of government by elected representatives, the effectiveness of the civil service and freedom from corruption; *democratic political culture,* which relates to social norms concerning democratic principles; and finally, *political participation,* which refers to the adult literacy rate, the percentage of women in Parliament, and the extent to which citizens can join political parties and freely choose elected representatives. In terms of our earlier discussions *democratic political culture* and *political participation* are measures of civil society, and the other indicators relate to the function and process of government and also to the legal framework in which democracy operates.

Table 9.1 shows the strength of the correlations, or measures of association, between the five indicators of democracy in the OECD countries. It is apparent that they are all very much connected with each other, although some correlations are larger than others. Civil liberties and electoral processes are highly associated and the strength of the relationship between political culture and political participation is weaker,

Table 9.1   Correlations between the Economist Intelligence Unit's components of the index of democracy in OECD countries

	Components of democracy	A	B	C	D	E
A	Electoral processes and pluralism	1.00				
B	Civil liberties	0.81	1.00			
C	Functioning of government	0.57	0.62	1.00		
D	Democratic political culture	0.58	0.72	0.72	1.00	
E	Political participation	0.63	0.62	0.77	0.70	1.00

Source: Quality of Governance Cross-Section Data, 2005; see http://www.qog.pol.gu.se.

though still significant. The functioning of government measure is quite
strongly linked to the two indicators of civil society, which confirms the
findings of Chapter 8 about the importance of civic engagement to the
effectiveness of government. Finally, political culture and political participation are closely associated as well.

Table 9.1 confirms the fact that if democracy is defined very broadly
to include measures of civil society as well as legal rights, electoral
processes and the effective functioning of government, then all of these
make important contributions to supporting effective democracy. Civil
society is closely related to the efficiency and fairness of democratic
government. The implication of these findings is that if civil society
starts to weaken then the effectiveness of other aspects of democracy
such as civil liberties, freedom from corruption, fair elections and effective government, are likely to weaken as well.

How does Britain rank on the different scales? The answer is not particularly well in relation to the other twenty-nine OECD countries.
Britain is ranked 9th on *electoral processes*, 21st on *civil liberties*, 12th
on the *functioning of government*, 16th on *democratic political culture*,
and 27th on *political participation*. The combined scale groups all of
the five together as shown in Figure 9.1 – Britain ranks 22nd on this
combined scale. The country is part of the group of 'Full Democracies',
but it is low down in the group. To put this in perspective, every country
in the rankings below Britain, with the exception of France, is categorized as a 'Flawed Democracy' a 'Hybrid Regime' or an 'Authoritarian
Regime'. Kekic explains why Britain is well down the list of full democracies in the following terms: 'In Britain low political participation (the
lowest in the developed world) is a major problem, and to a lesser
extent, for now, so are eroding civil liberties' (2007: 6)

In effect, Figure 9.1 confirms the earlier analysis in this book. British
democracy is beginning to show signs of strain and looks ineffective in

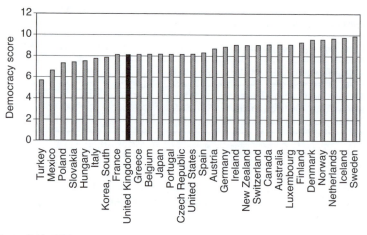

Source: Kekic, 2007.

Figure 9.1   Scores on the Economist Intelligence Unit index of democracy in OECD countries, 2006

many respects. This does not augur well for the Big Society initiative, although arguably it has arisen in response to an awareness that there are not enough people volunteering and citizens are not motivated enough to take political action at the local level. But what is the role of government in all of this? Is it a barrier to expanding voluntary activity, or does it play a part in building the Big Society? We address this issue next.

The 'invisible handshake' revisited

The central argument developed in this book is that in the modern state there needs to be a close relationship between the citizen and the government if democracy is to work properly. To reiterate points made earlier, the 'invisible handshake' means that citizens look to the state to protect and support them and, in exchange, they acknowledge their obligations to pay taxes, to obey the law, and to participate periodically in choosing the government. The demand for rights without the acknowledgment of obligations will weaken the state to the point that eventually democracy will break down. Therefore, the key to understanding the role of government in supporting civil society is to look at this relationship of mutual interests.

As we have observed, the state protects its citizens from external attack and internal disorder but this is something that all states have done throughout history. In fact, this is one of the defining characteristic of the state as a distinctive entity. However, the modern advanced industrial state tries to do much more than this. As the discussion in Chapter 7 showed, the modern state supplies merit goods and transfer payments, with the aim of correcting market failures and alleviating inequalities. If it did not, then educational provision would be inadequate, healthcare would be less than needed and widespread deprivation would characterize the lives of the poorest citizens. This, in turn, would have implications for internal order and also for the legitimacy of the state and the willingness of individuals to give their allegiance to it. This argument has been central to the justification of social policy ever since Bismarck introduced social welfare payments in the German Empire in the nineteenth century (Castles, 1989).

This idea has implications for the relationship between the state and civil society. If the invisible handshake actually works then it implies that generous provision of merit goods and the effective delivery of welfare should be closely related to the strength of civil society. A country which deals effectively with market failures by responding to its citizens' demand for welfare should also have a strong civil society. On the other hand, if a country is unresponsive to the needs of its citizens and does not effectively deliver benefits of this type, the sense of obligation of its citizens is likely to be weak, tax avoidance will be rife and political participation limited.

In the next section we examine the relationship between civil society and welfare provision more fully in order to understand the nature of the invisible handshake.

Civil society and welfare benefits

The relationship between welfare provision and civil society can be investigated using some of the indicators of civic attitudes, political participation and institutional affiliations examined in Chapter 7. The relationship between welfare indicators and measures of civic engagement will be examined using two different approaches. One approach is to look at the legal framework underpinning social welfare, or the legal responses to social needs such as provision for the elderly, the sick and the unemployment, which are written into statute law and into government regulations. The invisible handshake means that countries which

Table 9.2   Correlations between the indicators of civil society and the social security index in OECD countries (p < 0.05 = **)

Civil society indicator	Social security laws index
Government should take more responsibility	–0.15
Confidence in Parliament	0.53**
Political action index	0.51**
Interpersonal trust	0.53**

Source: Quality of Governance Cross-Section Data, 2005; see http://www.qog.pol.gu.se.

possess strong legal protections supporting the welfare of their citizens should also have healthy civil societies. A second approach to addressing the same issue is to look at the relationship between spending on social welfare and indicators of civil society. Legal requirements are important but they may not amount to very much if spending on welfare provision is limited. In other words, spending is vital to the enforcement of legal rights, and if the invisible handshake is working properly, then countries with high levels of welfare spending should also be countries where active civil societies can be found.

To examine the legal framework of welfare rights first, an investigation of labour market conditions across the world by Botero *et al.* (2004) looked at the extent to which the law supported social welfare provision in different countries. Their research involved the construction of a 'social security laws' index, which combined data on social benefits and welfare provision. Legally defined levels of social welfare relate to matters such as, old-age, disability, death, sickness and unemployment benefits (Botero *et al.* 2004: 1349). For example, old-age, disability, and death benefits, were measured as follows:

> The average of the following four normalized variables (1) the difference between retirement age and life expectancy at birth (2) the number of months of contributions or employment required for formal retirement by law (3) the percentage of the worker's monthly salary deducted by law to cover old-age, disability and death benefits, and (4) the percentage of the net pre-retirement salary covered by the net old-age cash-benefit pension. (Botero *et al.* 2004: 1349)

Table 9.2 shows the correlations between the four indicators of civil society used in Chapter 7 and the Botero social security laws index in OECD countries. It will be recalled that 'government responsibility'

Table 9.3   Correlations between the indicators of civil society and social security spending in OECD countries (p < 0.05 = **)

Civil society indicator	Social security spending as % GDP
Government should take more responsibility	−0.41**
Confidence in Parliament	0.40**
Political action index	0.39**
Interpersonal trust	0.26

Source: Quality of Governance Cross-Section Data, 2005; see http://www.qog.pol.gu.se

measured people's demand for government intervention to ensure that everyone is provided for; 'confidence in Parliament' captured attitudes to this key institution of democracy; the 'political action index' measures various types of participation other than voting; and 'interpersonal trust' is the most important indicator of social capital. Apart from the government responsibility variable there are strong positive relationships between the legal enforcement of social welfare benefits and civic engagement in OECD countries. If the citizens of a country have confidence in their legislature, are willing to participate in politics, and tend to trust each other, then those countries are likely to have strong legal protections for the elderly, the sick and the unemployed. This is the invisible handshake in action.

Table 9.3 looks at the other aspect of social protection, spending on social welfare in the OECD countries. This is measured by the percentage of each country's Gross Domestic Product spent on social protection. Once again, there are significant correlations between spending on welfare and the indicators of civil society, with the exception of interpersonal trust which is positively related to welfare but with a non-significant effect. This means that if citizens demand more state intervention, are willing to participate in politics and have confidence in their legislature then spending on social protection in their country is likely to be high. These relationships are rather similar to those in Table 9.2. This is not surprising since there is positive correlation (0.53) between spending on social protection and the legal provisions for such protection across OECD countries. Spending and legal protections go together and both are significantly associated with a healthy civic culture.

What then does this all mean for the Big Society initiative and the role of government in stimulating political participation and improving civil society? We consider this next.

What should government do?

In Chapter 7, we observed that the relationships between indicators of civil society and the Human Development Index were positive and significant, the implication being that if one could increase the health, knowledge and prosperity of citizens this would help to build civic engagement and create social capital. This in turn would help to make the 'Big Society' a reality. However, government finds it hard to prolong the life expectancy of individuals, promote the prosperity and to increase the knowledge of its citizens. Arguably, these are the long-term goals of most, if not all, policy initiatives taken by government, but they are likely to take a long time to come to fruition assuming that government can influence them at all. So we are left with the question: can government actually influence civil society to the extent of reversing the decline apparent in Britain and thereby lay the foundations of the Big Society initiative?

We have examined a wide range of evidence concerning the relationship between civil society, the policy-making process and government decision making. We have been careful to examine correlations rather than attempting to identify causal relationships. It is clear for example, that political participation is associated with the government delivery of welfare benefits, and also government effectiveness in general, but we cannot be sure if participation is driving delivery, or if the process works the other way round. Most probably it is an interaction between these different measures which would require a controlled experiment to identify and access to data, which is not currently available to researchers.

However, the evidence is strongly supportive of the argument that the state is a complement to civic engagement not a substitute for it. Thus the activities of the state support civil society and stimulate voluntarism rather than reduce it. If extensive legal regulation and high levels of spending on welfare were a substitute for voluntary activity, which is the implication of the 'substitute' or crowding out thesis, then we would observe negative correlations between these measures. That is, if the substitution argument applied, then countries with low levels of welfare spending would have high levels of voluntary activity and vice versa. Accordingly, the first implication of the findings for the Big Society programme is that a large-scale cut back in state support for welfare is likely to bring about a reduction in voluntary activity rather than an increase. There is no convincing evidence that the state 'crowds out' voluntary activity and political participation and, in fact, the evidence points in the opposite direction.

A moment of reflection highlights why this should be the case. As Chapter 7 showed, the state is heavily involved in welfare provision because it has historically responded to the demands of its citizens for additional spending. In Victorian times, the state stepped in precisely because charitable work and voluntary activity, though laudable in themselves, were inadequate to the task of providing for the needs of citizens in the new industrial society. If voluntary activity spontaneously arises when the state retreats from welfare provision, then one would have expected the nineteenth-century minimal state to have much more voluntary activity than the twentieth-century interventionist state. Though much philanthropy and charitable work was carried out in nineteenth-century Britain, there is no evidence to suggest that it was greater than in the twentieth century, and moreover it was inadequate to the task of dealing with the consequences of massive industrialization and urbanization.

The British government introduced the first significant welfare benefits in the first decade of the twentieth century when David Lloyd George, the Chancellor of the Exchequer in the Liberal government introduced social insurance and pensions for the first time. He borrowed extensively from the pioneering model of welfare introduced in Germany by Bismarck (Castles, 1989). It is interesting that Bismarck's initiative was undertaken precisely to promote the social and political cohesion of the newly established German Reich. In effect the world's first mass-welfare provision was an exercise in nation building. After Lloyd-George, the post-Second World War Labour government subsequently expanded welfare spending greatly when it implemented the recommendations of the Beveridge Report (1942) on the welfare state. As is well known, the report published at the height of the Second World War laid the groundwork for welfare provision in Britain for much of the post-war period. Subsequently, the welfare budget has grown rapidly under both Labour and Conservative governments in response to the needs of a complex modern democracy.

The implication of this is that large-scale cutbacks in welfare spending and in public services more generally are likely to damage civil society and undermine voluntary activity rather than have the opposite effect. So in response to the question: *what should government do?* the first point to make is that it should not cut welfare spending and public services to the level that this begins to happen. Savings can always be made in public expenditure and efficiency improved, but really deep cuts are likely to undermine the Big Society project rather than sustain it. In these circumstances the state runs the risk of removing essential services while at the same time undermining voluntary activity which would otherwise help to alleviate some of the effects of the cuts.

There is another important aspect of the Big Society programme and this relates to the devolution of power from the centre. If comparisons are made between Britain and other advanced industrial democracies such as the United States and Germany, the British state is highly over-centralized. Moreover such centralization appears to be against the trend occurring in a number of advanced industrial democracies in favour of devolution. Formerly highly centralized states such as Italy and Spain have radically devolved power to their regions and localities over the last quarter of a century, while at the same time the British state has been moving in the opposite direction (Esping-Andersen, *et al.*, 2002).

The one clear exception to this trend in centralization is the devolution of power to Scotland and to Wales which occurred after Labour was elected to government in 1997. But the process of devolution ended there, and the growth of quangoes responsive only to central government, the targets and indicators culture in the public sector introduced by New Labour, and the budget capping and Whitehall directives to local government have served only to centralize the system even more. There is a number of arguments for centralization that are frequently rehearsed to justify these policies. They are based on the notion that direction from the centre brings common standards, managerial efficiencies, economies of scale and reduces 'post-code lotteries' in the delivery of services.

However, there are significant counter-arguments to excessive centralization, namely that it stifles innovation, promotes bureaucratic rent-seeking, creates administrative complexity, burdens individuals with excessive regulation, and ignores local priorities. Despite extensive attempts to remove post-code lotteries in the delivery of services such as healthcare and education during the Labour government, they are just as prevalent today as they were in the 1990s. The key problem of centralization is that efficiencies are defeated by organizational complexity and bureaucratic rigidities. Local communities feel little ownership of policies which are imposed on them, and so in the case where policy implementation relies on civil society to be effective they are undermined by excessive centralization.

Figure 9.2 throws light on the debate about the advantages and disadvantages of centralization. The figure shows the relationship between the percentage of the budget spent at the sub-national level and government effectiveness in OECD countries. Budget spending at the sub-national level is a proxy measure of the extent to which a country has a

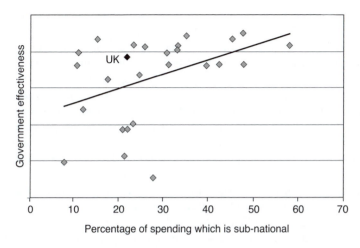

Percentage of spending which is sub-national

Source: Quality of Governance Cross-Section Data, 2005; see http://www.qog.pol.gu.se.

Figure 9.2   The relationship between the decentralization of spending and government effectiveness in OECD countries (correlation = +0.43)

relatively decentralized political system. If there is a great deal of decision making at the sub-national level it will be accompanied by equal amount of spending at that level. The government effectiveness measure was extensively examined in Chapter 7, and the correlation between the two variables is positive (+0.43) and statistically significant. Therefore, the figure suggests that political systems which devolve a good deal of decision making to the sub-national level are more effective than those that do not. Rather than centralization improving efficiency, it tends to reduce it.

Britain appears well below the average in the chart in terms of the decentralization of the state, with just over a fifth of the budget spent at the sub-national level. This is in sharp contrast to the United States where close to half the budget is spent at the state and local levels. Britain ranks eighteenth out of twenty-six countries in relation to the decentralization of the budget and much of this is due to devolution to Scotland, Wales and Northern Ireland. If Britain were judged purely in terms of decentralization of power to local government in England, it would be even closer to the bottom of the list.

One of the surprising features of the Big Society programme is that it does not mention local government. It advocates the devolution of power and decision making down to the local level, but directly to citizens rather than to local elected representatives. In this respect it perpetuates a long tradition of British statecraft, that of ignoring or trying to marginalize local government (Cochrane, 1993: Sullivan, 2003). This is a very curious phenomenon since local government is an obvious ally in helping to revitalize civil society. We examined the relationship between decentralization and government effectiveness in Figure 9.2, but there is also a significant positive correlation between government spending at the sub-national level and interpersonal trust (0.49), the key measure of social capital. Societies with high levels of social capital also tend to have relatively decentralized political systems, which would indicate that thriving local government both encourages and, at the same time is stimulated by, high levels of social capital. Therefore, removing local control over policies by centralization, bypassing local government, and appointing unelected bodies or self-selected groups of citizens is likely to weaken social capital.

There is survey evidence in Britain that citizens are more satisfied with the services provided by local government such as libraries, street cleaning and sports facilities than they are with those provided by the national government. After reviewing this evidence Pattie, Seyd and Whiteley concluded that: 'The public prefers service providers to be local rather than national' (2004: 113). As we observed in Chapter 2, satisfaction with government delivery of national policies is fairly low, and is a further reason to be critical of the argument that a centralized state delivers efficient outcomes.

The implication of these findings is that a revival of local government and the elective principal at the local level should be part of the Big Society programme. Additional local volunteering is only likely to come about in partnership with local government, rather than in opposition to it. A revival of local government means changing the tax system so that a far higher percentage of local government revenues are raised locally rather than provided by central government. An equitable way to do this would be via local income or sales taxes, rather than the unpopular and inequitable council tax. As long as the great majority of local government expenditure is financed from central government grants, it is never going to be a robust and independent source of enhanced local political activity and a source of democratic legitimacy. Since the Second World War the proportion of revenues raised from taxation at the local level has declined sharply (Clarke and Dilnot, 2002). This is the clearest indicator of the decline in local government. Restoring this with the aim of reviving local government is an important part of the task of rebuilding civil society.

Up to this point, we have been examining government activities and policy making, and changes will not be easy to make as they are at odds with much contemporary Conservative thinking about the desirability of government shrinking in size in response to the economic crisis. But government does control budgets and can change the legal status of local government, and is therefore in a position to make these changes. However, there are more fundamental forces at work in bringing about the weakening of civil society, which government will find much harder to change. In particular, the gradual growth of inequality in Britain is one of the key factors in explaining these trends, and this is discussed next.

Inequality and civil society

We observed in Chapter 7 that inequality is harmful for the effectiveness of government but, in their important book, Wilkinson and Pickett (2009) show how inequality has a malign effect on many aspects of modern life, including health, life expectancy, obesity, interpersonal trust, educational performance, crime and social mobility. They argue:

> [M]ost of the important health and social problems of the rich world are more common in more unequal societies... Problems are anything from three times to ten times as common in the more unequal societies. (Wilkinson and Pickett, 2009:173)

Inequality within societies matters, because when citizens compare themselves with others this can generate a strong sense of relative deprivation in very unequal societies. Relative deprivation arises when individuals perceive that they are losing out in relation to income, wealth, opportunities and in social mobility in comparison with their fellow citizens – it is the gap between what individuals expect out of life and what they actually experience (Runciman, 1966; Walker and Smith, 2002). These comparisons are likely to be unfavourable in very unequal societies if large differences exist between their own circumstances and those of their fellow citizens.

The focus of Wilkinson and Pickett's research is very much on issues relating to health and individual welfare, although they did examine interpersonal trust, a question we have looked at extensively in relation to social capital. Their findings showed that interpersonal trust is weaker in more unequal societies (Wilkinson and Pickett, 2009: 52–3). They

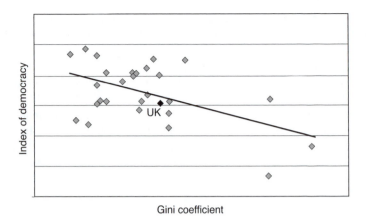

Source: Quality of Governance Cross-Section Data, 2005; see http://www.qog.pol.gu.se

Figure 9.3   The relationship between the index of democracy and income inequality in OECD countries, 2005 (correlation = –0.52)

did not examine political participation and civic engagement in any detail, and so it is interesting to explore how these key indicators of civil society are affected by inequality. Figure 9.3 examines the relationship between the Gini coefficient, the measure of income inequality, and the Index of Democracy or the combined measure of political participation, civic engagement and system performance which appear in Figure 9.1.

Figure 9.3 shows that there as a very significant negative relationship between the index of democracy and income inequality across OECD countries. The correlation between these measures is –0.52, which shows that higher inequality is associated with lower civic engagement, poorer system performance and lower rates of political participation. Thus the dysfunctional characteristics of unequal societies identified by Wilkinson and Pickett extend to democracy and civic engagement. In one sense this is not surprising, since if inequality generates poor health, unhappiness, extra crime, lower educational performance and increased mental health problems, then it is quite likely to cause weakened civic ties, reduced voluntary activity and lower rates of political participation.

Figure 9.3 suggests that inequality is damaging for civil society. But to explain the weakening of civic ties examined in earlier chapters, we need to look at trends over time. There is annual time series data available on income inequality for Britain and is shown in Figure 9.4 which examines trends over a forty-five-year period from 1961 to 2006. The

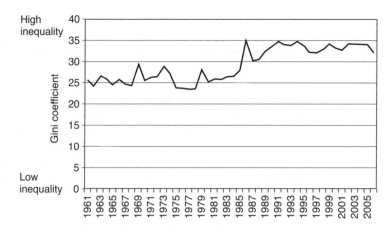

Source: Quality of Governance Time Series Data; see http://www.qog.pol.gu.se.

Figure 9.4 Trends in inequality in Britain, 1961–2006

chart shows that income inequality in Britain has risen by just over a third during this period, although the trend rise has not been uniform. The Conservative government under Prime Minister Harold Macmillan left office in 1964 and was replaced by Harold Wilson's Labour government in the general election of that year. That government started out with ambitious objectives but ran into severe economic problems by 1967–8 (Whiteley, 1983: 131–48). One of the consequences of the deflationary policies that it pursued was a rise in inequality, as Figure 9.4 shows. The subsequent and relatively short-lived Conservative administration of Edward Heath was also associated with an increase in inequality between 1970 and 1974, but thereafter inequality fell during the period of the mid to late 1970s. This was during the Wilson–Callaghan Labour government of 1974 to 1979, which introduced a number of policies aimed at reducing inequality even though it was a minority government for much of the time (Whiteley, 1983). In fact, the years 1977 to 1979 represent the low point of income inequality during this forty-five year period.

A Conservative government was elected in 1979 with Mrs Thatcher as Prime Minister and although she was replaced by John Major in 1990, the Conservatives were re-elected four times between then and 1997. This eighteen-year period enabled the Conservative governments to entrench a number of policies which promoted inequality, such as tax

cuts, privatization policies, and spending reductions in key welfare programmes. As a result, a step change in inequality occurred after 1980,
reflecting in part the tremendous growth in corporate income inequality,
particularly in the City of London, but also a relative reduction in key
social benefits over time. For example, one key decision was to break
the link between the growth of pensions and the growth of incomes and
instead link pensions to the retail price index. This occurred in 1981 and
it meant that pensioners were compensated for inflation, but did not
share in the growth of the prosperity of the wider economy (Whiteley,
1986). As a consequence the value of pensions eroded over time and
income inequality increased.

The arrival of New Labour in office in 1997, with a very large majority, produced a decade of economic growth and rising prosperity along
with electoral success for the party (Clarke *et al.*, 2004; 2009). However,
it did nothing to reduce the income inequality which had built up over
the previous eighteen years. While it is true that income inequality did
not rise further during the Labour government, the Gini index was little
changed between 1997 and 2006. Initiatives, such as the minimum wage
and changes to taxation, served to prevent the further growth of inequality but they were not sufficiently radical to reduce it during this period.

These trends highlight one important factor in the decline of civil
society charted earlier, the growth of inequality in British society over
time. If citizens are increasingly separated from each other by a widen-
ing social and economic gulf, then they are less likely to identify with
each other to feel a common sense of community and to want to cooperate in pursuing collective goals. In short inequality erodes citizenship.

Conclusion

This chapter has examined the relationship between civil society, the
policy-making process and policy outcomes and it shows that there are
close links between effective governance, equality and civil society.
There is no convincing evidence that downsizing the public sector will
boost the voluntary sector, and in fact the evidence tends to support the
opposite conclusion. If the Big Society initiative is to be successful,
therefore, the Coalition government will have to restrain cuts in public
expenditure and will need to continue sustaining the welfare state. The
issue of inequality is difficult for governments to address, though it
appears to have a powerful effect on civic engagement and the effectiveness of government. The Institute for Fiscal Studies, an influential

think-tank, suggested in a report after the 2010 Budget that the effects of the budget will be regressive and a significant burden resulting from the changes will fall upon the poorest groups in society (Browne and Levell, 2010). If this trend in fiscal policy making continues, the likelihood is that the Coalition government will weaken civil society and this in turn will undermine the Big Society project.

Trends in civic engagement over time are relatively easy to ignore by governments, since as we have seen, they are not very well charted by available data with the exception of electoral participation. Equally, changes in civil society tend to be slow in comparison with the changes in other social and economic indicators, such as GDP or government spending. The short-term perspective that governments have, partly driven by electoral considerations but also by the sheer pressure of events, makes long-term policy making difficult. Hence, it is easy for governments to ignore the decline of civil society, or to believe that it does not really matter as far as effective government is concerned. This view is profoundly mistaken.

Some of the evidence discussed in earlier chapters suggests that governments are failing to deliver effective policies where the public are concerned, and this is producing a declining demand for government services over time. One solution to this trend is to radically downsize government to make it tax and spend much less. However, it is premature to think that disillusionment with policy delivery provides an opening for parties which advocate such policies. This is because the source of these opinions is not disillusionment with government *per se* but rather discontent with the present institutions of the British political system, which, for reasons discussed in this book, do not deliver what they promise.

As we have seen, for many people Parliament does not work very well, the political parties are declining, policy making is often ill-conceived and badly implemented and public accountability is weak. Above all the sense of efficacy of the average citizen is low, and this is because it is very hard to influence the highly centralized British political system. If a political party were to convince the electorate that it could revitalize the institutions of the state and make them more efficient and accountable and that as a result government would work much more effectively, then it would probably win a general election. In other words there is a clear difference between wanting less government and wanting less ineffective government.

This book has shown that civic engagement has declined significantly over time in Britain to the point that it has started to damage British democracy. Perhaps one of the most disturbing findings relates to the Economist Intelligence Unit's Index of Democracy, which shows that Britain is on the edge of being relegated from the premier league of being a 'Full Democracy' to the category of a 'Flawed Democracy', alongside countries such as Italy, Slovakia and Mexico. If this happens, it will be the product of taking for granted the health of the civic culture and ignoring the warning signs from falling turnouts in elections, the decline in the prestige and relevance of Parliament, and the withering away of political parties at the grassroots level. Can a country sleepwalk into losing its democratic institutions and healthy civic culture? Only time will tell if it can.

Bibliography

Alesina, A., D. Carloni and G. Lecce (2010) 'The Electoral Consequences of Large Fiscal Adjustments' (unpublished manuscript, Harvard University).

Almond, G. and S.Verba (1963) *The Civic Culture: Political Attitudes and Democracy in Five Nations* (Princeton: Princeton University Press).

Ansolabehere, S. and S. Iyengar (1995) *Going Negative* (New York: The Free Press).

APSA (American Political Science Association) (1950) 'Towards a More Responsible Two-Party System', *American Political Science Review,* 44, supplement.

Arrow, K. (1972) 'Gifts and Exchanges', *Philosophy and Public Affairs*, 1: 343–62.

Atkinson, A. B., L. Rainwater and T. M. Smeeding (1995) *Income Distribution in OECD Countries* (Paris: OECD).

Bache, I. and S. George (2006) *Politics in the European Union* (Oxford: Oxford University Press).

Barber, B. (1984) *Strong Democracy* (Berkeley, CA: University of California Press).

Barnes, S. H., M. Kaase *et al.* (1979) *Political Action: Mass Participation in Five Western Democracies* (Beverly Hills: Sage Publications).

Barratt, C. (2008) *Trade Union Membership 2008* London: Department of Business, Enterprise and Regulatory Reform).

Baumol, W. J. (1967) *Welfare Economics and the Theory of the State* (Cambridge MA: Harvard University Press).

Beer, Samuel (1965) *Modern British Politics* (London: Faber).

Beer, Samuel (1982) *Britain Against Itself* (London: Faber).

BES (various years) Continuous Monitoring Survey of the British Election Study, see http://bes2009-10.org

Bevan, Aneurin (1952) *In Place of Fear* (London: Heinemann).

Beveridge, W. (1942) *Social Insurance and Allied Services* (Cmnd 6404) (London: HMSO).

Birch, A. H. (1964) *Representative and Responsible Government* (London: Allen and Unwin).

Black, D. (1958) *Theory of Committees and Elections* (Cambridge: Cambridge University Press).

Bobbio, Norbeto (1989) *Democracy and Dictatorship* (Cambridge: Polity Press).

Borcherding, T. E. (1977) *Budgets and Bureaucrats: The Sources of Government Growth* (Durham: Duke University Press).

Borcherding, T. E. and R. T. Deacon (1972) 'The Demand for the Services of Non-Federal Governments', *American Economic Review,* 62: 891–901.

Botero, J. C., S. Djankov, R. La Porta, F. Lopez-de-Silanes, and A.Shleifer (2004) 'The Regulation of Labor', *Quarterly Journal of Economics*, vol. 119, no. 4: 1339–82.

Brady, H., S. Verba and K.Schlozman (1995) 'Beyond SES: A Resource Model of Political Participation', *American Political Science Review*, 89: 271–94.

Brehm, J. and W. Rahn (1997) 'Individual-Level Evidence for The Causes and Consequences of Social Capital', *American Journal of Political Science,* 41: 888–1023.

Brennan, G. and J. Buchanan (1980) *The Power to Tax: Analytical Foundations of a Fiscal Constitution* (Cambridge: Cambridge University Press).

Brody, R. (1978) 'The Puzzle of Political Participation in America' in A. King (ed.), *The New American Political System* (Washington, DC: American Enterprise Institute).

Browne, J. and P. Levell (2010) 'The Distributional Effect of Tax and Benefit Reforms to be Introduced between June 2010 and April 2014: A Revised Assessment', *IFS Briefing Note 108* (London: Institute for Fiscal Studies).

Buchanan, J. M. and R.E. Wagner (1977) *Democracy in Deficit* (New York: Academic Press).

Butler, D. and G. Butler. (2006) *British Political Facts since 1979* (London: Palgrave Macmillan).

Butler, D. and R. Rose (1959) *The General Election of 1959* (London: Macmillan).

Butler, D. and D. Stokes (1974) *Political Change in Britain: Forces Shaping Electoral Choice*, 2nd edn (London: Macmillan).

Cameron, David (2010) 'David Cameron Launches Tories' "Big Society" Plan', http://www.bbc.co.uk/news/uk-10680062, accessed 25 August, 2010.

Capella, J. N. and K. H. Jamieson (1994) 'Broadcast Adwatch Effects: A Field Experiment', *Communication Research,* 21: 342–65.

Capella, J. N. and K. H. Jamieson (1997) *Spiral of Cynicism: The Press and the Public Good* (New York: Oxford University Press).

Castles, F. (ed.) (1989) *The Comparative History of Public Policy* (London: Polity Press).

Castles, F. (ed.) (2007) *The Disappearing State: Retrenchment Realities in an Age of Globalisation* (London: Edward Elgar).

Claibourn, M. P. and P. S. Martin (2000) 'Trusting and Joining? An Empirical Test of the Reciprocal Nature of Social Capital', *Political Behavior*, 22: 267–91.

Clarke, H. D., D.Sanders, M.C. Stewart and P. Whiteley (2004) *Political Choice in Britain* (Oxford: Oxford University Press).

Clarke, H. D., D. Sanders, M.C. Stewart, and P. Whiteley (2009) *Performance Politics and the British Voter* (Cambridge: Cambridge University Press).

Clarke, P. B. (1996) *Deep Citizenship* (London: Pluto Press).

Clarke, T. and A. Dilnot (2002) *Long-Term Trends in British Taxation and Spending. Briefing Note 25* (London: Institute for Fiscal Studies).

Cochrane, A. (1993) *Whatever Happened to Local Government* (Buckingham: Open University Press).

Coleman, J. (1988) 'Social Capital in the Creation of Human Capital', *American Journal of Sociology,* 94, supplement S95–S119.

Coleman, J. (1990) *Foundations of Social Theory* (Cambridge, MA: Belknap Press of Harvard University Press).

Cowley, P. (ed.) (1998) *Conscience and Parliament* (London: Frank Cass).

Cowley, P. (2002) *Revolts and Rebellions: Parliamentary Voting under Blair* (London: Politico).

Cowley, P. (2005) *The Rebels: How Blair Mislaid his Majority* (London: Politico).

Dahl, R. A. (1956) *A Preface to Democratic Theory* (Chicago: University of Chicago Press).

Dahl, R. A. (1971) *Polyarchy: Participation and Opposition* (New Haven CT: Yale University Press).

Dahl, R. A. (1989) *Democracy and Its Critics* (New Haven CT: Yale University Press).

Dalton, R. J. (2005) *Citizen Politics* (Washington, DC: Congressional Quarterly Press).

De Tocqueville, A. (1990) *Democracy in America, Vol. 1* (New York: Vintage Books).

Deacon, R. (2006) *Devolution in Britain Today* (Manchester: Manchester University Press).

Denters, B. (2002) 'Size and Political Trust: Evidence from Denmark, the Netherlands, Norway, and the United Kingdom', *Environment and Planning C: Government and Policy*, 20, 793–812.

Denver, D. (2003) *Elections and Voters in Britain* (London: Palgrave Macmillan).

Denver, D. and G. Hands (1997) *Modern Constituency Electioneering* (London: Frank Cass).

Downs, A. (1957) *An Economic Theory of Democracy* (New York: Harper & Row).

Dowse, R.A. and J. A. Hughes (1977) 'Sporadic Interventionists', *Political Studies*, 25 (1):84–92.

Dunn, J. (1992) *Democracy: The Unfinished Journey, 508 BC to AD 1993* (Oxford: Oxford University Press).

Easterly, W. R. (2001) 'The Lost Decades: Developing Countries' Stagnation in Spite of Policy Reform 1980-1998', *Journal of Economic Growth*, 6 (2): 135–57.

Edwards, B. and M. W. Foley (1998) 'Civil Society and Social Capital beyond Putnam' *American Behavioral Scientist*, 42 (1): 124–39.

Esping-Andersen, G., D. Gallie, A. Hemerijck and J. Miles (2002) *Why We Need a New Welfare State* (Oxford: Oxford University Press).

European Social Survey (various years), see http://www.europeansocialsurvey. org/.

Ferri, E., J. Bynner and M. Wadsworth (2003) *Changing Britain, Changing Lives* (London: Institute of Education).

Frandsen, A. G. (2002) 'Size and Electoral Participation in Local Elections', *Environment and Planning C: Government and Policy*, 20, 853–69.

Franklin, M. (1985) *The Decline of Class Voting in Britain* (Oxford: Oxford University Press).

Franklin, M. (2004) *Voter Turnout and the Dynamics of Electoral Competition* (Cambridge: Cambridge University Press).

Fridkin, K. L. and Kenney, P. J. (2004) 'Do Negative Messages Work? The Impact of Negativity on Citizens' Evaluations of Candidates', *American Politics Research*, 32, 570–606.

Fukuyama, F. (1995) *Trust: The Social Virtues and the Creation of Prosperity* (London: Hamish Hamilton).

Gerbner, G., L. Gross, M. Morgan and N. Signorielli (1980) 'The "Mainstreaming" of America: Violence Profile No. 11', *Journal of Communication,* 30, 3: 10–29.

Gigerenzer, G. and P. M. Todd (1999) *Simple Heuristics That Make Us Smart* (Oxford: Oxford University Press).

Glaeser, E. L. and B. Sacerdote (2000) 'The Social Consequences of Housing', *Journal of Housing Economics,* 9 (1–2):1–23.

Gouveia, M. and N.A. Masia (1998) 'Does the Median Voter Explain the Size of Government?: Evidence from the States', *Public Choice,* 97: 159–77.

Granovetter, M. (1973) 'The Strength of Weak Ties', *American Journal of Sociology,* vol 78: 1360–80.

Grenier, P. and K. Wright (2001) 'Social Capital in Britain: An Update and Critique of Hall's Analysis', paper presented at ARNOVA's 30th Annual Conference, 29 November to 1 December.

Hall, P. (1999) 'Social Capital in Britain', *British Journal of Political Science,* 29, 3: 417–62.

Halpern, David (2005) *Social Capital* (London: Polity Press).

Held, D. (1996) *Models of Democracy* (London: Polity Press).

Hirsch, F. (1976) *Social Limits to Growth* (Cambridge, MA: Harvard University Press).

HMSO (1976) *The Report of the Committee on Financial Aid to Political Parties.*

Holcombe, R. G. (1994) *The Economic Foundations of Government* (New York: New York University Press).

Holcombe, R. G. (2005) 'Government Growth in the Twenty-First Century', *Public Choice,* 124: 95–114.

Inglehart, R. (1997) *Modernization and Post-Modernization* (Princeton: Princeton University Press).

Inglehart, R. (1999) 'Trust, Well-Being and Democracy' in Mark E. Warren (ed.), *Democracy and Trust* (Cambridge: Cambridge University Press).

ISSP (International Social Survey Programme) (1985–2006) *Role of Government Surveys,* see http://www.issp.org/.

ISSP (International Social Survey Programme) (2004) *Citizenship Survey,* see http://www.issp.org/

Iversen, T. (2005) *Capitalism, Democracy and Welfare* (Cambridge: Cambridge University Press).

Iversen, T. (2006) 'Electoral Institutions and the Politics of Coalitions: Why Some Democracies Redistribute More Than Others', *American Political Science Review,* 100, no. 2: 165–81.

Iversen, T. and D. Soskice (2006) 'Electoral Institutions and the Politics of Coalitions: why some democracies redistribute more than others', *American Political Science Review,* 100: 165–81.

Iyengar, S. (1991) *Is Anyone Responsible? How Television Frames Political Issues* (Chicago: University of Chicago Press).

Johnston, R. and C. Pattie (1995) 'The Impact of Spending on Party Constituency Campaigns at Recent British General Elections', *Party Politics,* 1: 261–73.

Judge, D. (1993) *The Parliamentary State* (London: Sage).

Judge, D. (1999) *Representation: Theory and Practice in Britain* (London: Routledge).

Kau, J. B. and P. H. Rubin (1981) 'The Size of Government', *Public Choice*. 37(2): 261–74.

Kaufmann, D., A.Kray and M. Mastruzzi (2006) *Governance Matters V: Aggregate and Individual Governance Indicators for 1996–2005* (Washington DC: The World Bank).

Kavanagh, D. (1980) 'Political Culture in Britain: The Decline of the Civic Culture' in G. A. Almond and S. Verba (eds) *The Civic Culture Revisited* (London: Sage).

Kavanagh, D. and P. Cowley (2010) *The British General Election of 2010* (London: Palgrave Macmillan).

Kawachi, I. and L.F. Berkman (2000) 'Social Cohesion, Social Capital and Health' in L. F. Berkman and I. Kawachi (eds) *Social Epidemiology* (Oxford: Oxford University Press).

Kekic, L. (2007) *The Economist Intelligence Unit's Index of Democracy* (London: The Economist Intelligence Unit).

Kinder, D. R. and R. D. Kiewiet (1981) 'Sociotropic Politics: The American Case', *British Journal of Political Science*, 11:129–61.

King, A. R., J. Wybrow and A. Gallup (2000) *British Political Opinion 1937–2000* (London: Politico).

Klingemann, H. D., I. Budge and J. Barro (2006) *Mapping Policy Preferences II* (Oxford: Oxford University Press).

Knack, S. (2002) 'Social Capital and the Quality of Government: Evidence from the States', *American Journal of Political Science*, 46: 772–85.

Knack, S. and P. Keefer (1997) 'Does Social Capital Have an Economic Payoff? A Cross-Country Investigation', *The Quarterly Journal of Economics*, 112: 1251–88.

Kristoff, L., P. Lindert and R. McClelland (1992)'Pressure Groups and Redistribution', *Journal of Public Economics*, 48: 135–63.

Lasswell, H. (1936) *Politics:Who Gets What, When and How* (New York: McGraw-Hill).

Lijphart, A. (1977) *Democracy in Plural Society* (New Haven, Conn: Yale University Press).

Lin, N. and B. H. Erickson (2010) *Social Capital: An International Research Programme* (Oxford: Oxford University Press).

Lipsky, Michael (1980) *Street Level Bureaucracy. Dilemmas of the Individual in Public Services* (New York: Russell Sage Foundation).

Luft, Oliver (2010) 'ABCs: *Times* drops below 500,000 as all titles suffer falls', http://www.pressgazette.co.uk/ accessed 1/10/2010.

Meltzer, A. H. and S. F. Richard (1978) 'Why Government Grows (and Grows) in a Democracy' *Public Interest*, 52: 111–18.

Meltzer, A. H. and S. F. Richard (1981) 'A Rational Theory of the Size of Government', *Journal of Political Economy*, 89: 914–27.

Meltzer, A. H. and S. F. Richard (1983.)'Tests of a Rational Theory of the Size of Government', *Public Choice*, 41 (3): 403–18.

Middlemas, K. (1986) *Power, Competition and the State* (London: Macmillan).

Milner, Henry (2002) *Civic Literacy: How Informed Citizens Make Democracy Work* (Hanover: University of New England Press).

Mueller, D. C. (2003) *Public Choice III* (Cambridge: Cambridge University Press).

Mueller, D. C. and P. Murrell (1986) 'Interest Groups and the Size of Government', *Public Choice,* 48: 125–45.

Musgrave, R. A. (1959) *The Theory of Public Finance* (New York: McGraw-Hill).

Mutz, Diana C. (1998) *Impersonal Influence: How Perceptions of Mass Collectives Affect Political Attitudes* (Cambridge: Cambridge University Press).

Newton, K. (1999) 'Social and Political Trust in Established Democracies', in Pippa Norris (ed.) *Critical Citizens* (Oxford: Oxford University Press).

Newton, K. and P. Norris (2000) 'Confidence in Public Institutions: Faith, Culture or Performance?' in Susan Pharr and Robert D Putnam (eds) *Disaffected Democracies: What's Troubling the Trilateral Democracies?* (Princeton, NJ: Princeton University Press).

Nie, N. H., J. Junn and K. Stehlik-Barry (1996) *Education and Democratic Citizenship in America* (Chicago: University of Chicago Press).

Niskanen, W. A. (1971) *Bureaucracy and Representative Government* (Chicago: Aldine-Atherton).

Norris, P. (1996) 'Does Television Erode Social Capital? A Reply to Putnam', *PS: Political Science and Politics,* 29.

Norris, P. (ed.) (1999) *Critical Citizens* (Oxford: Oxford University Press).

Norris, P. (2000) *A Virtuous Circle: Political Communications in Postindustrial Societies* (Cambridge: Cambridge University Press).

Norris, P., J. Curtice, D. Sanders, M. Scammell and H. A. Semetko (1999) *On Message: Communicating the Campaign* (London: Sage).

OECD (2009) http://www.oecd.org.

Oliver, Eric (2000) 'City Size and Civic Involvement in Metropolitan America', *American Political Science Review,* 94: 361–73.

Oliver, Eric (2001) *Democracy in Suburbia* (Princeton NJ: Princeton University Press.)

Olson, M. (1965) *The Logic of Collective Action* (Cambridge MA: Harvard University Press).

Olson, M. (1982) *The Rise and Decline of Nations: Economic Growth, Stagflation and Social Rigidities* (New Haven: Yale University Press).

Parry, G., G. Moyser and N. Day (1992) *Political Participation and Democracy in Britain* (Cambridge: Cambridge University Press).

Pattie, C., P. Seyd and P.F. Whiteley (2004) *Citizenship in Britain: Values, Participation and Democracy* (Cambridge: Cambridge University Press).

Peacock, A. T. and J.Wiseman (1961) *The Growth of Public Expenditure in the United Kingdom* (Princeton, NJ: Princeton University Press).

Peltzman, S. (1980) 'The Growth of Government', *Journal of Law and Economics,* 23: 209–88.

Persson, T. and G.Tabellini (1999) 'The Size and Scope of Government: Comparative Politics with Rational Politicians', *European Economic Review,* 43: 699–735.

Platte, S. (ed.) (1991) *Respectfully Quoted: A Dictionary of Quotations* (New York: Barnes and Noble).

Portes, A. (1998) 'Social Capital: Its Origins and Applications in Modern Sociology', *Annual Review of Sociology*, 24: 1–24.

Power to the People (2006) *The Report of the Power Commission: An Independent Inquiry into Britain's Democracy* (London: Power Commission).

Przeworski, A. (1991) *Democracy and the Market* (Cambridge: Cambridge University Press).

Pulzer, P. (1967) *Political Representation and Elections* (London: Macmillan).

Putnam, R. (1993) *Making Democracy Work: Civic Traditions in Modern Italy* (Princeton: Princeton University Press).

Putnam, R. (1995) 'Tuning In, Tuning Out: The Strange Disappearance of Social Capital in America', *PS: Political Science and Politics*, 28: 664–83.

Putnam, R. (2000) *Bowling Alone: The Collapse and Revival of American Community* (New York: Simon & Schuster).

Rice, T.W. (1986) 'The Determinants of Western European Government Growth, 1950–1980', *Comparative Political Studies*, 19: 233–57.

Rodrik, D. (1998) 'Why Do More Open Economies Have Bigger Governments?' *Journal of Political Economy*, 106 (5): 997–1032.

Romer, T. and H. Rosenthal (1979) 'Bureaucrats versus Voters: On the Political Economy of Resource Allocation by Direct Democracy, *Quarterly Journal of Economics*, 93: 563–87.

Ronis, D. L. and E. R. Lipinski (1985) 'Value and Uncertainty as Weighting Factors in Impression Formation', *Journal of Experimental Social Psychology*, 21: 47–60.

Runciman, W. G. (1966) *Relative Deprivation and Social Justice* (Berkeley, CA: The University of California Press).

Saegert, S. G. and G. Winkel (1998) 'Social capital and the revitalization of New York City's low-income housing', *Housing Policy Debate*, (9) 1: 17–60.

Samuelson, P. (1954) 'The Pure Theory of Public Expenditure', *Review of Economics and Statistics*, 36: 387–89.

Sanders, D. and N. Gavin (2004) 'Television News, Economic Perceptions and Political Preferences in Britain, 1997–2001, *Journal of Politics*, 66: 1245–66.

Sarlvik, B. and I. Crewe (1983) *Decade of Dealignment: The Conservative Victory of 1970 and Electoral Trends in the 1970s* (Cambridge: Cambridge University Press).

Scarrow, S.E. (1996) *Parties and Their Members* (Oxford University Press).

Seyd, P. and P.Whiteley (1992) *Labour's Grassroots: The Politics of Party Membership* (Oxford: Oxford University Press).

Seyd, P. and P.Whiteley (2002) *New Labour's Grassroots: The Transformation of the Labour Party Membership* (London: Palgrave Macmillan).

Sherman, R. (2008) *Market Regulation* (Boston: Pearson/Addison-Wesley).

Slemrod, J. and J. Bakija (2004) *Taxing Ourselves: A Citizen's Guide to the Debate over Taxes* (Cambridge MA: The MIT Press).

Smith, M. (1999) *The Core Executive in Britain* (London: Macmillan).

Soroka, S. (2006) 'Good News and Bad News: Asymmetric Responses to Economic Information', *Journal of Politics*, 68: 372–85.

Stigler, G. J. (1971) 'The Theory of Economic Regulation', *Bell Journal of Economics and Management Science,* 2: 137–46.

Sullivan, H. (2003) 'Local Government Reform in Great Britain', in N. Kersting and A. Vetter (eds) *Reforming Local Government in Europe* (Opladen, Germany: Leske and Budrich) pp. 39–64.

Sundquist, James L. (1981) *The Decline and Resurgence of Congress* (Washington, DC: The Brookings Institution).

Tanzi, V. and L. Schuknecht (2000) *Public Spending in the 20th Century* (Cambridge: Cambridge University Press).

Tarrow, Sidney, (1996) 'Making Social Science Work across Space and Time: A Critical Reflection on Robert Putnam's Making Democracy Work', *American Political Science Review*, 90: 389–97.

Teorell, J., M. Samanni, Nicholas Charron, Sören Holmberg and Bo Rothstein (2010) 'The Quality of Government Dataset', version 27 May 2010 (University of Gothenburg: The Quality of Government Institute), http://www.qog.pol.gu.se.

Thomassen, J. (ed.) (2004) *The European Voter* (Oxford: Oxford University Press).

Van Deth, J., M. Marraffi, K. Newton and P. Whiteley (eds) (1999) *Social Capital and European Democracy* (London: Routledge).

Verba, S. and N. H. Nie (1972) *Participation in America* (Chicago: University of Chicago Press).

Verba, S., N. H. Nie and J.O. Kim (1978) *Participation and Political Equality: A Seven Nation Comparison* (Cambridge: Cambridge University Press).

Verba, S., K. Schlozman and H. E. Brady (1995) *Voice and Equality: Civic Voluntarism in American Politics* (Cambridge, MA: Harvard University Press).

Walker, I. and H. Smith (eds) (2002) *Relative Deprivation: Specification, Development and Integration* (Cambridge: Cambridge University Press).

Webb, P. (2000) *The Modern British Party System* (London: Sage).

Weir, S. and D. Beetham (1999) *Political Power and Democratic Control in Britain: The Democratic Audit of the United Kingdom* (London: Routledge).

Whiteley, P. F. (1983) *The Labour Party in Crisis* (London: Methuen).

Whiteley, P. F. (1986) *Political Control of the Macroeconomy* (London: Sage).

Whiteley, P. (1999) 'The Origins of Social Capital' in J. Van Deth, M. Marraffi, K. Newton and P. Whiteley (eds) *Social Capital and European Democracy* (London: Routledge).

Whiteley, P. (2000) 'Economic Growth and Social Capital', *Political Studies* 48, 3: 443–66.

Whiteley, P. (2009) 'Where Have All the Members Gone? The Dynamics of Party Membership in Britain', *Parliamentary Affairs*, vol. 62, no. 2: 242–57.

Whiteley, P., H. D. Clarke, D. Sanders and M. Stewart (2010) 'Government Performance and Life Satisfaction in Contemporary Britain', *Journal of Politics,* vol. 72, no. 3: 733–46.

Whiteley, P. and P. Seyd (2002) *High Intensity Participation – The Dynamics of Party Activism in Britain* (Michigan, MI: University of Michigan Press).

Whiteley, P., P. Seyd and A. Billinghurst (2006) *Third Force Politics: Liberal Democrats at the Grassroots* (Oxford: Oxford University Press).

Whiteley, P., P. Seyd and J. Richardson (1994) *True Blues: The Politics of Conservative Party Membership* (Oxford: Oxford University Press).

Whiteley, P. F. and S. Winyard (1986) *Pressure for the Poor: The Poverty Lobby and Policy-Making* (London: Methuen).

Wilkinson, R. and K. Pickett (2009) *The Spirit Level: Why Equality is Better for Everyone* (London: Penguin Books).

Winter, S. and P. E. Mouritzen (2001) 'Why People Want Something for Nothing: The Role of Asymmetric Illusion', *European Journal of Political Research*, vol. 39: 109–43.

Zaller, J. (1996) 'The Myth of Massive Media Impact Revived: New Support for a Discredited Idea', in D. Mutz, P. Sniderman and R. Brody (eds) *Political Persuasion and Attitude Change* (Ann Arbor, MI: University of Michigan Press) 17–78.

Index